T0271019

THE R. M. JONES LECTURES IN THE DEVELOPMENT OF IDEAS

People, food and resources

The current problems of sub-Saharan peoples who are subject to recurrent famine and shortages of food are only one facet of a wider problem which confronts the peoples of the world. This problem, which is vast in scale, concerns the relationship between the physical and biological resources which the world can muster and the provision of food for the adequate nutrition of its peoples. Overshadowing much of the thought about the future is the theorem propounded by Malthus almost 200 years ago, namely that population, unless checked in some way, has the capacity to outstrip the productivity of the earth in supplying food. Malthus' views are examined in this book and estimates are made of the need to increase and the possibilities of increasing both the nutritional status of the world's population and the production of food and other essentials. The enormous dilemmas that face mankind, the economic arguments that, while apparently logical, pose large moral questions, and the possible role of new scientific advances are outlined. The likely solutions to the many and vexed problems are analysed and the urgency of them emphasised.

The book is a definitive account of the problems of meeting world needs for food, both now and in the immediate future, discussed dispassionately and analytically. It is based on public lectures given by the author in the Queen's University of Belfast in 1984.

People, food and resources

Sir KENNETH BLAXTER F.R.S.

CAMBRIDGE UNIVERSITY PRESS

Cambridge

New York   Port Chester

Melbourne   Sydney

CAMBRIDGE UNIVERSITY PRESS
Cambridge, New York, Melbourne, Madrid, Cape Town,
Singapore, São Paulo, Delhi, Tokyo, Mexico City

Cambridge University Press
The Edinburgh Building, Cambridge CB2 8RU, UK

Published in the United States of America by Cambridge University Press, New York

www.cambridge.org
Information on this title: www.cambridge.org/9780521323000

First published 1986
Reprinted 1987,1988,1989,1991

A catalogue record for this publication is available from the British Library

Library of Congress Cataloguing in Publication Data

Blaxter, Sir Kenneth
People, food and resources.
(The R. M. Jones Lectures in the development of ideas)
Bibliography: p.
Includes index.
1. Food supply. 2. Population. I. Title. II. Series
HD9000.5.B514 1986 338.1'9 85-26941

ISBN 978-0-521-32300-0 Hardback

Contents

List of figures

Tables

Preface

A bequest was made to the Queen's University of Belfast in accordance with the will of the late Robert Millar Jones to the effect that its Vice Chancellor and Senate should arrange courses of lectures at intervals of three years. The lectures were to be specifically concerned with major themes in the intellectual history of the sciences, social sciences and humanities and were to be known as 'The R. M. Jones Lectures in the Development of Ideas'. This book stems from the lectures which I was invited to give in the spring of 1984 under the terms of the bequest.

The arrangements made for the lectures are of considerable interest. Following each one (and after an excellent dinner) a colloquium is held. Present are members of the University interested in the subject matter and scholars whom the University invites to participate. These colloquia are of very great value, not least to the lecturer, for they enable aspects of the subject to be explored in more depth than is possible in the lecture itself. The lecturer can indeed revise the manuscripts of his lectures with the benefit of much constructive criticism and thought. I am most grateful to all those who took part in these discussions and particularly to Sir Charles Periera, former Chief Scientist of the Ministry of Agriculture, Fisheries and Food of the UK, to Dr I. D. Carruthers, Reader in Agrarian Development, School of Rural Economy and Related Studies, Wye College, University of London, to Dr W. Jack, Permanent Secretary of the Department of Agriculture, Northern Ireland and to Dr D. H. Shrimpton, Director General of the British Nutrition Foundation, London. Their comments, based on their considerable expertise, have been most valuable.

At these colloquia it is usual for the Vice Chancellor to act as chairman and Dr Peter Froggatt not only undertook this task of preventing academic argument becoming too remote, but equally contributed much in terms of wise comment. As well as being greatly indebted to the Queen's University and honoured by their invitation, I am equally indebted to him for his many kindnesses to me during my visit to Belfast.

Stradbroke Hall, Stradbroke, Suffolk KENNETH BLAXTER

1

Introduction

During the last few decades concern has been increasingly expressed about the growth in the number of people in the world and questions have been raised about whether the resources that we can muster to increase the production of food and other essentials on which man depends are sufficient to keep pace with a burgeoning humanity. In the early 1970s the reports by the Club of Rome, in which mathematical methods of dynamic modelling were used to elucidate the relations between population growth, industrialisation, the use of natural resources and pollutional effects of man's activities, suggested that, ultimately, catastrophe was inevitable (Meadows *et al.*, 1972; Mesarovic and Pestel, 1974). At this same time, however, there was a far more immediate concern about the food supplies of the world. In 1971, 1972 and 1973 a combination of poor harvests in each of the major grain-producing areas of the world, combined with the policy change made by the government of the United States of America to reduce its reserve stocks, led not only to increases in grain prices, but to a realisation that the world was critically dependent on each year's harvest. The increase in price had devastating effects on poorer countries which of necessity had to import grain to feed their peoples. The World Food Conference was called by the Food and Agriculture Organisation (FAO) of the United Nations in November 1974 to discuss this serious and immediate problem. At its end the 127 member states, who for the most part were represented by their heads or senior ministers, proclaimed that 'Within one decade no child will go to bed hungry, no family will fear for its next day's bread and no human being's future and capabilities will be stunted by malnutrition.' No doubt the participants believed that this goal could be reached by 1984. Plainly, it has not. Illustrative are events in Ethiopia, Somalia and other countries in North Africa and East Africa. In 1973, and contributing to international concern, there was famine in Ethiopia following the failure of the long rains of the previous June to September (Miller and Holt, 1975). Now, a more prolonged partial failure of the rains has taken place and again, ten years later, famine has taken a toll of life. Furthermore, there is no reason to believe that in many of the less well developed countries of the world the supplies of food per head of the population is any greater than it was a decade ago; indeed in many it is less.

The statement made at the end of the World Food Conference can perhaps best be interpreted, either as one of hope or one of resolve, and it was brave to make it. That these hopes have not been fulfilled or the resolve translated into an accomplishment is sad. The failure, however, does focus attention on the difficulties that surround the vast problems of the relationships between the numbers of mankind, the food and other essentials that people require and the resources on which the production of these essentials depend. In the chapters which follow some of these problems are described together with the ideas of many who have studied them and suggested possible solutions. Finally, my views are given about what currently seem to be the most sensible courses of action to follow in seeking ways to achieve, not simply a freedom from hunger but also a more equitable world.

Inevitably, the approach adopted involves the making of predictions about what might happen in the future if particular courses of action were to be taken or if present courses were to continue unchanged. The reliability of such predictions warrants thought. Most predictions entail an extrapolation from past experience. However well summarised or generalised this experience may be, it is not infallible and extrapolation is necessarily fraught with error. This is particularly so in the biological and social sciences which are those which are largely our concern. Identification of all the determinants and their interactions is rarely complete and freedom from extraneous factors seldom attainable. Thus even the most plausible and seemingly well-founded hypotheses lead to predictions that have an intrinsic uncertainty.

A more relevant consideration concerns how predictions should be used. When, at some future time, we look back we will discern but one past, whatever the way in which we might then interpret it. It must follow that there can be but one future. The current value of forecasts of that future resides not so much on their precise prediction of what will occur as on their prediction of what might occur. Consideration of these possible futures allows us to take action so to avoid any adverse consequences that might ensue. Thinking about the future through the formulation of predictive hypotheses can thus prompt action and change thought. I imagine – but do not know – that many of the latter-day Cassandras who predict doom and destruction for mankind are well aware of this constructive aspect of future studies. They may also think that the more frightening the vista of the future they present, the greater will be the reaction and the more forceful the action to avoid what they predict. I have attempted to avoid overstatement of the seriousness of our current predicament; it is already serious enough.

2

The numbers of people

MALTHUS

Any discussion about the growth of the population of the world must begin with Thomas Robert Malthus. It was the rejection of a then current view about the future that prompted Malthus to write his famous essay which he published anonymously in 1798. His purpose was to refute what he regarded as an unwarranted idealism about the perfectibility of human society, an idealism that probably had its roots in the revolution in France. The title of the essay indeed reflects this underlying purpose and is: *An Essay on the Principle of Population as it affects the Future Improvement of Society, with Remarks on the Speculations of Mr Goodwin, M. Condorcet and Other Writers.*

In the essay Malthus attempted to explain the apparent stability or, at the most, the slow growth of human populations and used the 'principle' he formulated as the basis of a critique of the idealistic hypotheses. Malthus had been a student at Jesus College, Cambridge, where he had studied mathematics and he presented his principle in these terms. He began by stating his postulates: 'first that food is necessary to the existence of man and secondly that the passion between the sexes is necessary and will remain nearly in its present state'. He then stated: 'Assuming these postulates as granted, I say that the power of population is indefinitely greater than the power of earth to produce subsistence for man. Population, when unchecked, increases in a geometrical ratio. Subsistence increases only in an arithmetical ratio.'

One might immediately cavil at Malthus' logic. His postulates do not lead to his conclusions; he simply states his principle as his opinion. He continued, however, and here he displayed the customary condescension of the mathematically minded: 'A slight aquaintance with numbers will show the immensity of the first power in comparison with the second.' Malthus then added that to achieve stability of population in these circumstances 'implies a strong and consistently operating check on population from the difficulty of subsistence'. He identified this check as twofold; first a positive check 'which in any degree contributes to shorten the natural duration of life' and second a 'preventative check' which included all those factors which prevent human birth. And, finally, to clinch the argument and to point his attack on Goodwin and the idealists, Malthus wrote: 'it is difficult to conceive of any check on population that does not come under the description of misery and vice'. While Malthus gave some examples of these positive checks to illustrate his thesis, Grigg (1980) has pointed out that none of them related to the curtailment of reproduction by insufficiency of food. This is true not only of his original essay of 1798 but also of the more extended account which he wrote in 1803 and which went through four editions.

THE EARLY CRITICISM

The kernel of Malthus' principle has been given through quotations from his book largely because there are few works which have been so extensively misinterpreted. For example, in a Cabinet Office paper concerned with the transfer of resources to the countries of the developing world (1976) it was stated that 'unless transfers take place on a scale many times greater than at present, the effective check to world population will be the Malthusian trilogy of war, pestilence and famine'. Malthus' primary checks were two, the positive check and the preventative check, although in a later work *A Summary View of the Principle of Population* (1830) one can discern three secondary ones – vice, misery, and moral restraint. Certainly he did not regard three of the four horsemen as the checks involved. Flew in his essay on Malthus (1970) gives other examples of misinterpretation; some of these are such that the views attributed to Malthus are the antithesis of those which he expressed so clearly in his work.

In the early part of the nineteenth century, however, Malthus' essay had clearly been read and understood. It caused an immense controversy. This controversy largely surrounded the final phase of his overall argument, namely that in the last analysis human populations are controlled by misery and vice. What Malthus had done was to state in logical terms a fatalism and a pessimism which effectively absolved the ruling classes in England from any responsibility for the ever-increasing numbers of the poor. He had attacked the emerging idealism and liberal ideas as exemplified by the Poor Laws and he stated quite categorically: 'Hard as it may seem in individual instances, dependent poverty ought to be held disgraceful. A stimulus seems to be necessary to promote the happiness of the great mass of mankind and general attempts to weaken this stimulus, however benevolent its apparent intention, will always defeat its own purpose.' As J. M. Keynes expressed it in an address on the centenary of Malthus' death: 'the principle provided a powerful intellectual foundation to justify the status quo, to ward off experiments and to keep us all in order'.

The first criticisms, even allowing for the freedom of expression of the time, were vituperative and malicious. Cobbett, the political and agricultural commentator, wrote: 'I have during my life detested many men; but never any one as much as you . . . No assemblage of words can give an appropriate designation of you; and, therefore, as being the single word which best suits the character of such a man I call you "Parson", which among other meanings includes that of Borough-Monger' (Cobbett, 1819). It was, no doubt, this passage that in after years earned for Malthus the soubriquet, 'the gloomy clergyman', and for the corollary to his principle, namely that population equilibrium is only achieved at the expense of misery and vice, the term 'the dismal theorem'. William Hazlitt, the essayist, in a very long critique of Malthus published in 1825, put forward as a base for ridicule a second corollary to the principle, known as 'the utterly dismal theorem'. This corollary is that any increase in the level of food production in the world must increase the total sum of human vice and misery because population will inevitably increase until Malthus' checks become operant.

Much of the initial reaction to the essay was, however, fragmented and more concerned with the political consequences of Malthus' views in relation to the depression which followed the Napoleonic wars. Many aspects of this early debate were summarised by Smith (1951). Later, more polished rebuttals appeared and these attempted to refute Malthus' principle argument, but most of these have not survived in terms of an assimilation into modern thought. In 1830 Sadler published an enormous work with the incredible title: *The Law of Population: A Treatise in Six Books; in Disproof of the Superfecundity of Human Beings and Developing the Real Principle of Their Increase: in Two Volumes*. In this Sadler stated his own law, namely: 'The prolificness of human beings, otherwise similarly circumstanced varies inversely as their numbers.' He indeed thought that urbanisation would result in a reduction of population and that a reduction in the rate of increase in the numbers of people 'is affectuated not by the wretchedness and misery but by the happiness and prosperity of the species'. Doubleday (1847) went even further. He postulated that fecundity would diminish with the development of individual talents. He wrote: 'Most of the flat-chested girls who survive their high-pressure education are incompetent to bear a well-developed infant and to supply that infant with the natural food for the natural period.' Education, and particularly high-pressure university education would surely solve the Malthusian paradox. These views expressed by Sadler and Doubleday in some ways anticipate those accepted in the twentieth century in support of the so-called demographic transition theory which will be discussed later.

The early socialists were obviously in considerable opposition to Malthus' views for the reasons already given, and they also attacked the man for lack of originality. Marx accused Malthus of plagiarism stating that he had done nothing more than cobble together the ideas of others including those of Robert Wallace (1753), Joseph Townsend (1786) and James Steuart (1767). Marx could have been even more scathing for Aristotle had expressed doubts about population growth in relation to land area centuries before. It might equally be argued that Marx himself had been guilty of borrowing ideas for the accusation he made was first put forward by William Hazlitt in a letter entitled 'On the originality of Mr. Malthus' principle argument'. In this he commented on Wallace's contribution. The publications of Townsend, Wallace and Steuart had certainly predated that of Malthus; and the accusation would have been justified if Malthus had not acknowledged an indebtedness. He wrote that his principle 'has been advanced and applied to the present subject, though not with its present might or in the forcible point of view by Mr. Wallace, and it may have been stated by many writers I have never met with'. Wallace had indeed reached Malthus' conclusion and so too had James Steuart Denby.

JAMES STEUART

James Steuart's contribution is particularly interesting. Steuart was a Scot, educated in Edinburgh and a Jacobite. He was not at the final battle on Culloden Moor since, at the request of Lord George Murray, he was attempting to bring about a French invasion of England in order to relieve the pressure exerted by General Wade's forces. After the defeat he was exiled to France although he escaped the Attainder. He was only pardoned in 1772, five years after publication of his work. Steuart had certainly anticipated Malthus for he wrote: 'The numbers of mankind must depend on the quantity of food produced by the earth for their nourishment, from which as corollary: That mankind have been as to numbers and must ever be in proportion to the food produced; and that food will be in the compound proportion of the fertility of the climate and the industry of the inhabitants.'

Steuart did not write well. He was regarded by the Hanoverian English as a traitor; he lived across the Channel for most of his life. It is little wonder that his work was largely ignored. Nevertheless, because of his emphasis on the value of state intervention in economic affairs, he should perhaps be regarded as the first Keynesian, and as Skinner (1966) has pointed out, his work bears comparison with that of Adam Smith who was his contemporary. He certainly predated Malthus in his views about population and its equilibrium and appears to have been a much nicer and less gloomy individual.

MALTHUS' ALGEBRA OF POPULATION GROWTH

It seems highly probable that the ideas which Malthus embodied in his essay were extant at the time he wrote it; certainly he has been given most credit for them. There is no doubt, however, that he was responsible for their expression in a mathematical form and it is pertinent to examine these aspects. In this respect one should heed the comment made by Hazlitt – 'mathematical terms carry with them an imposing air of accuracy and profundity and ought therefore, to be applied strictly and with the greatest caution, or not at all'! Perhaps this remark was the forerunner of other remarks in our own century such as 'lies, damn lies and statistics' or that associated with computer models – 'garbage in, garbage out'; Hazlitt's is certainly more elegantly phrased.

The dynamics of populations has been much studied by theoretical ecologists, as well as by demographers, and their work is apposite to the formulation and extension of Malthus' argument. The basic equation of population studies is:

$$\frac{dN}{dt} = N(b - d - e + i)$$

where dN/dt is the rate at which the population, N, increases with time, t; b is the birth rate; d the death rate; e the rate of emigration and i the rate of immigration, all these rates being expressed per person per unit time. For a population with no migration this reduces to:

$$\frac{dN}{dt} = N(b - d)$$

or

$$\frac{dN}{dt} = rN$$

where r is the rate of natural increase (or decrease) in the population. If as Malthus supposed r is a constant, invariant with time for an 'unfettered' population, then the population will grow exponentially, or, as Malthus expressed it, in geometrical ratio, because integration of the equation gives:

$$N(t) = N(t_o)\, e^{rt}$$

This is the first of Malthus' basic relationships: the second will be dealt with later. Mathematically, the integrated equation has some interesting properties. Firstly, not only does the size of the population grow exponentially (geometrically) but so too does the number added in each interval of time. Secondly, and not so immediately obvious, the last term is less than the sum of all previous terms. Thus if we take Malthus' simple geometrical progression, doubling the number in each succeeding interval to give the series 1, 2, 4, 8, 16, 32, ... etc., the sum of all the terms other than the last is always less than the last term. If exponential growth had occurred since the time of Adam and Eve, then there are more people alive today than have ever lived, or, if one does not accept the implied view of creation, since *Homo sapiens* emerged as a separate species. While this conclusion for exponential growth at a constant rate is mathematically correct, there is much evidence to show that it does not reflect what has happened during the course of history. Cook (1962) calculated that 65,000 million people were born between 6000 BC and 1962. At the latter date world population was only 3000 million. Thatcher's (1984) calculations using what are perhaps better estimates, showed that 58,000 million people had died in the interval from 40,000 BC to the present day. Thatcher's studies of the records of deaths in the United Kingdom from 1837 when the censuses began show that 73 million people have died since then. Our current population is 56 million. These figures for the United Kingdom are of high accuracy and can hardly be assailed. The fact that they do not accord with the premise that its population has grown exponentially at a constant rate simply means that the premise of constancy cannot be true and that the natural rate of increase, *r*, has changed over time.

PREDICTIONS FROM MALTHUS' EQUATION

One must, however, be fair to Malthus. He stated that population 'when unchecked' increases exponentially; he did not say that populations normally do so. In the later editions of his work, *A Summary View of the Principle of Population*, he attempted to estimate what the rate of increase in population would be if there were no checks upon it, that is to estimate the value of *r* in the equation for 'unfettered' growth. He used the population censuses from the former American Colonies, now the United States of America for his calculations, stating that this population was unlikely to have been limited by resources. After correcting for immigrants he found that the population doubled in about 25 years. This corresponds to a value of *r* of 0.0277 or 2.8% per annum, deriving from the fact that the doubling time of a population is the natural logarithm of 2 (0.693) divided by *r*. He contrasted this unfettered rate of growth of human populations with those he derived for Ireland, England and Europe where the values of *r* were 0.014 corresponding to doubling times of about 50 years.

If we take Malthus' coefficient of 0.0277 and the census figure of 3.16 million for the number of inhabitants of the USA in 1800, then the population of that country could be expected to be 516 million in 1984. In fact it is only 223 million and is growing at a rate which is only about a quarter of that which Malthus thought was unfettered. Clearly unfettered growth has not ensued in the 184-year period. There is no evidence to suggest that this decline in growth rate has come about through any lack of food; America has for long been the granary of the world. Nor is there much evidence of misery and vice of the nature that Malthus propounded. Similarly in Great Britain the enumeration of the population in 1801 was 10.9 million and Malthus estimated it to be growing at a rate that doubled it in 49 years. Now population should be 146 million rather than the present 56 million. Clearly unfettered growth, or growth constrained to a constant level, has not occurred. It is little wonder that the mathematical corollary to the exponential equation, namely that the living in the world outnumber all the dead, can be shown to be incorrect. The rates of natural increase of populations are not constants but variables.

The same conclusion emerges when consideration is given to the population of the world. Table 1 gives the population of the world at intervals from 5000 BC. It derives from the French demographer Biraben's analysis of all relevant material (Biraben, 1979) together with recent United Nations' data. Table 1 also shows the rates of natural increase of the world's population in successive periods and these demonstrate that the rate has been by no means constant. The mean rate of natural increase in the thousand years from 400 BC to AD 600 was 0.024% ($100 \times r$) implying that the doubling time of the population was then about 2900 years. In the subsequent 1000 years the rate was 0.103%, and the doubling time of the population was then 672 years. During the period from 1600 to 1900 the rate again increased to 0.345% and doubling time fell to 201 years. From 1900 to the present day the calculated rate of natural increase has been 1.243% implying a doubling time of only 55 years. These broad divisions, however, include periods when the rate of growth was considerably above the average and some periods

Table 1 *Estimates of world population and rates of natural increase from 5000 BC to the present*

Date	Population (millions)	% rate of natural increase between this date and the one previous*	Mean % rate during the period specified and doubling time
BC 5000	40	—	
1600	70	0.016	
800	100	0.044	
400	162	0.121	From 400 BC to
200	231	0.177	AD 600
AD 1	255	0.049	Rate = 0.024
200	256	0.002	Doubling time
400	206	−0.109	2,888 years
600	206	0.000	
700	207	0.005	
800	224	0.079	
900	226	0.009	From AD 600
1000	254	0.116	to AD 1600
1100	301	0.170	Rate = 0.103
1200	400	0.284	Doubling time
1300	432	0.076	672 years
1400	374	−0.144	
1500	460	0.206	
1600	579	0.230	
1700	679	0.159	From AD 1600 to
1750	770	0.251	AD 1900
1800	954	0.148	Rate = 0.346
1850	1241	0.506	Doubling time
1900	1633	0.549	201 years
1950	2513	0.852	From 1900 to 1980
1980	4415	1.878	Rate = 1.243
			Doubling time
			56 years

*$\% \text{ rate} = 100 \times \dfrac{\text{difference in natural logarithms of population}}{\text{difference in dates}}$

during which it was negative. Certainly there is no evidence of long-term stability in the rate of natural increase of the population of the world.

CURRENT POPULATION GROWTH

Recognising that rates of natural increase of population vary from time to time, it is nevertheless informative to consider current rates in the countries which make up the United Nations' family. These are summarised by region and by countries in different development stages in Table 2. This table shows that in Europe as a whole, including the Eastern European countries, population growth is slow, much slower than that in North America or in the Soviet Union. In the less well developed regions of the world the rate of growth is about three times that in the more developed ones. In Figure 1 the broad classifications given in Table 2 are shown in more detail in relation to both Malthus' estimate of unfettered population growth and that for population equilibrium. Some countries in Europe now have populations which are static or declining; some countries in Africa and Central America have populations which are growing at rates which are far greater than those which Malthus regarded as one that occurred when 'room and nourishment were most abundant' and when 'natural progress is not checked by the difficulty of procuring the means of subsistence'. Several individual countries, it will be noted from Figure 1, have rates of natural increase estimated to be in excess of 3.5% per annum, entailing a doubling of population in 18 to 20 years, always assuming that these rates continue unchanged. Such rates have only rarely been observed in the past. Humboldt's studies of births and deaths in Spanish America were used by Malthus to calculate a doubling time of that population of 19 years, it is true, but none of the scanty evidence about population growth in Europe suggests that such high rates of natural increase have ever been encountered before. In passing, it may be calculated that the limit to population growth rate is probably in the region

Table 2 *Estimates of birth rates, death rates and rates of natural increase of population in different regions of the world*

	Birth rate (/1000)	Death rate (/1000)	Rate of natural increase (%)	Years to double population
More developed regions				
Europe	14	10	0.4	176
North America	16	8	0.7	98
USSR	18	10	0.8	82
All more developed regions	16	9	0.6	111
Less developed regions				
Africa	46	17	2.9	24
Asia	28	11	1.8	39
Latin America	34	8	2.6	26
All less developed regions	32	12	2.0	34
World	28	11	1.7	41

of a doubling in 6 years. The calculation assumes that women commence reproductive life at 15 years of age, continue until aged 45, that they produce a child every year and that mortality of the children is minimal.

THE ACCURACY OF POPULATION ESTIMATES

In view of Hazlitt's comment about the imposing air of accuracy that surrounds numerical information, it is reasonable to enquire about the accuracy of estimates of population and of population growth. The extremely high estimates of current growth rates of populations in some of the less well developed countries of the world might suggest that, since they have to be based on enumeration of the whole population, they could be in error. In

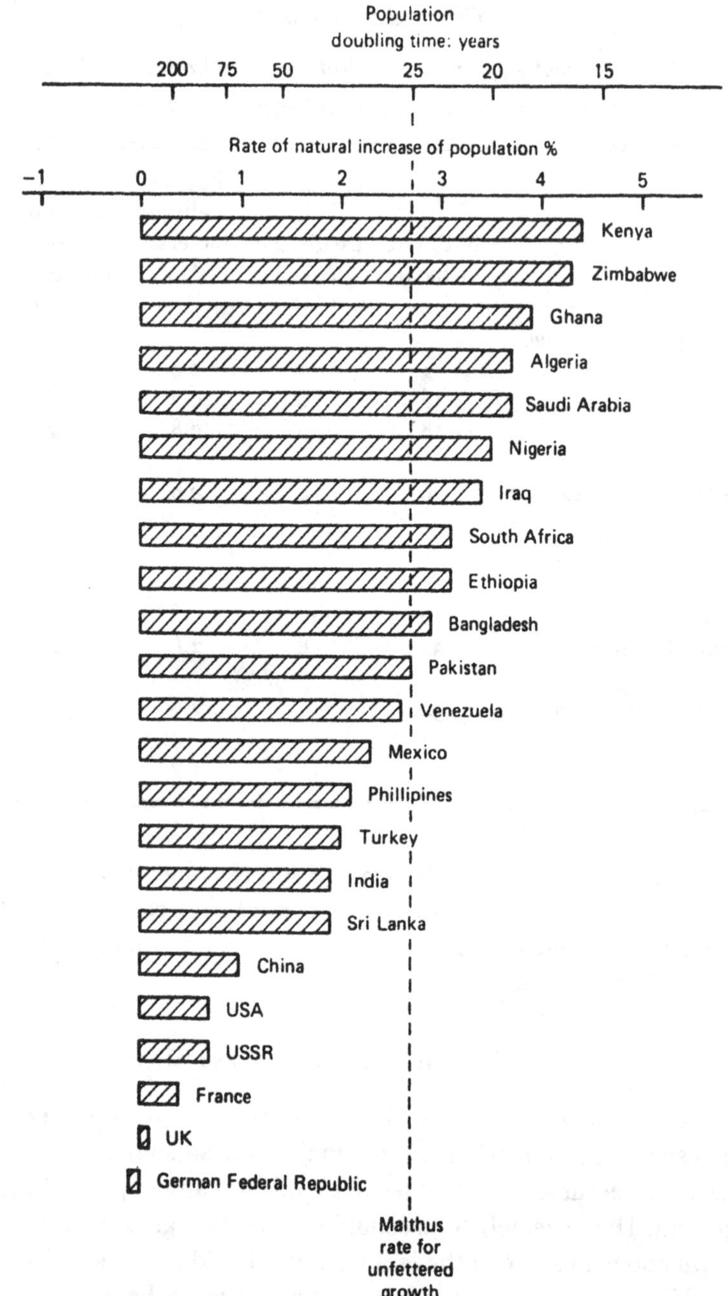

Figure 1 The rate of natural increase of populations in selected countries of the world. The vertical line represents that rate of natural increase which Malthus regarded as 'unfettered' by resource limitation.

the developed countries of the world a census is a relatively simple matter to conduct, though it entails considerable organisation; in the less well developed ones, counting the number of people and assessing their marital status is fraught with difficulty. The story of the censuses in Nigeria has been well documented (Caldwell and Okougie, 1968) and is illustrative of the problems. Apart from the difficulties of counting the migrant peoples – the Fulani herdsmen and the Hausa labourers – problems occurred which were referrable in part to the illiteracy or partial literacy of some of the enumerating staff. Furthermore, the population gained the impression that the enumeration was to be used to compile a new tax register and believed that it had political ends. The 1952 census was suspect immediately because very heavy rains made some roads impassible and some localities were not visited. The 1962 census was abandoned because of criticism of its inaccuracy and presumptive political bias, while the 1963 census which replaced it gave results which were not internally consistent. Similar problems have been encountered in other African countries, notably the Sudan and Sierra Leone.

In addition, there are considerable problems in developing countries over such commonplace matters as the recording of births and deaths – matters which are taken for granted in the developed countries of the world. Often the registration of births and deaths is restricted to towns and large settlements and the rates in rural areas have, of necessity, to be estimated. Even so, even though the raw data are not ideal or of the same precision as those obtained in the developed countries, there is no reason to believe that they are grossly in error, or inaccurate to such extent that they necessitate modification of the conclusion that the rate of increase of the populations in the developing countries of the world is considerably greater than that in the developed ones.

DEATH RATE, BIRTH RATE AND THE HUMAN DILEMMA

Table 2 shows that while the crude death rate in the less well developed countries of the world is only about a third greater than that in the developed ones, the crude birth rate is double. The rate of natural increase reflects the difference between the two and clearly in many of the less well developed countries population is far from equilibrium. It is of importance to consider population equilibrium without attributing any causal factors to its attainment. A stable population is defined by the value of *r* in what can be called Malthus' first equation being equal to zero, that is birth rate and death rate are then equal. Stability can be achieved at any birth rate provided it is equalled by the death rate. In the early fifteenth century in Europe, when there was evidence of some stability of the population, both death rate and birth rate were about 35 per 1000. Expectation of life at birth was about 30 years. In modern times no countries have yet reached a true stability of population since the age structures of their populations are not yet stable, although their crude rates of natural increase show no increase in numbers. Stability could well be achieved if death rates and birth rates were 13 per 1000. Expectation of life at birth would then be in excess of 75 years (Coale, 1974).

These considerations, which are quite independent of any related to the ways in which the numbers of people are or can be controlled, point forcibly to the dilemma of mankind. If we cling to life, if we all wish to live to a ripe old age, when biological factors related to the aging process rather than to potentially preventable disease curtails existence, then either reproduction rate must be diminished or we are committed to a continuing process of population expansion and the pressure of ourselves and our confreres on the resources of the world. This dilemma can be regarded as an example of an external diseconomy, in that health and related sexual activities of the individual may not be in the best interests of society as a whole. Adam Smith's concept that every individual, in pursuing his own selfish ends is led 'as if by an invisible hand' to achieve the best good for all certainly does not apply in this sphere of resource economics. Aspects of resource economics will, however, be dealt with in a later chapter.

MALTHUS' SECOND ASSERTION

We have so far dealt with one of the assertions that Malthus made, namely that related to the geometrical growth of population. The second part of his principle, namely that 'subsistence increases only in an arithmetical ratio', can also be expressed algebraically. A simple statement of his view is that the number of people supported by a given resource of land is increased year-by-year by a constant number. This leads to the equation:

$$N'(t) = N'(t_o) + bt$$

Where $N'(t)$ is the number of people a land resource can support at time, t; $N'(t_0)$ is the number supported initially and b is the number of additional people the resource can support each year. The equilibrium population is that when the number of people is equal to the carrying capacity of the land, that is when:

$$N(t_o)\,e^{rt} = N'(t_o) + bt$$

This equation can be solved numerically or graphically and a graph of the two functions is shown in Figure 2. The course of population growth increases exponentially until a specific point when it increases at a rate which is commensurate with carrying capacity.

This representation of population growth is not particularly elegant; population is unlikely to exhibit such a sudden change in course. A more reasonable assumption is that in some way numbers of people adjust in proportion to the pressure they exert on the land resource. Mathematical ecologists and population dynamicists have long been familiar with such types of population regulation and the simplest form of a relationship that still embodies Malthus' ideas is probably that first proposed by Verhulst. Instead of Malthus' two differential equations:

$$\frac{dN}{dt} = rN \text{ and } \frac{dN'}{dt} = b$$

in which r is a constant rate of increase of the population, this rate can be modified continuously and reduced downwards as the

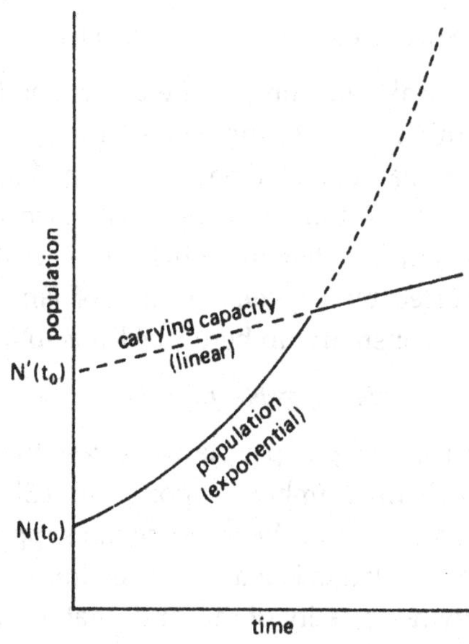

Figure 2 A graphical representation of Malthus' algebra. Population growth is 'geometrical', that is exponential. The means of subsistence is 'arithmetical', that is the number of people supported on an area increases linearly.

population approaches the maximal carrying capacity of the land resource. This maximal carrying capacity of the land resource can be regarded as a constant, K. The rate of increase of the population is then multiplied by a factor which is the proportion of carrying capacity that has not been realised at any particular time, that is:

$$\frac{(K - N)}{K} \text{ or } 1 - \frac{N}{K}$$

This leads to the differential equation:

$$\frac{dN}{dt} = N\,r\left(1 - \frac{N}{K}\right)$$

and its solution is:

$$N(t) = \frac{K}{1 + \frac{K - N(t_o)}{N(t_o)} e^{-rt}}$$

or equivalently:

$$N(t) = \frac{K}{1 + e^{-r(t-t^*)}}$$

Where $N(t_0)$ is the number in the population at the starting time of t, and in the alternative form the time scale corrects for the arbitrary time of origin. The work of Piclou (1977) and of Causton (1977) can be consulted for fuller accounts of the algebraic manipulations involved.

The above equation leads to sigmoid growth of population with a mid point at which the curve turns over. Population then slowly approaches the maximum through a reduction of the intrinsic rate of increase, r. The relationship embodies the idea of an approach of population to a maximum value dictated by resources and it is usually known as the logistic equation or the Pearl–Verhulst equation, the latter because Pearl employed it extensively in his studies of biological populations.

The logistic equation can be modified. As it is it states that population growth rate adjusts instantaneously according to its proximity to the limit. It is more sensible to insert a time delay in this adjustment; after all the pressure on the resource exerted by an infant, wholly dependent on its mother does not become apparent until that infant grows. If a time delay is inserted the differential equation becomes:

$$dN = N\, r\, (1 - \frac{N(t - t')}{K}$$

Here the factor modifying the intrinsic rate of increase, r, involves $(t - t')$ that is the time t' years or days previous (depending on the time scales adopted). This equation has some interesting properties which have been thoroughly explored by May (1973; 1975). If the delay term is large then the population overshoots the carrying capacity and it then oscillates about the carrying capacity in a series of predictable ways. Such behaviour is very common in cybernetics and in control system technology and the population oscillations are fully analogous.

Other equations of greater complexity have been devised, involving further assumptions about how the primary intrinsic rate of natural increase is modified. Most of them can be justified by appeals to experimental populations of bacteria, protozoa and simple animal species, notably insects (Williamson, 1974). The concepts they embody include an approach of population to a maximum rather than to an intersection as with Malthus' two expressions and they do not alter his concept in any really major fashion. They simply express it in what perhaps is a more realistic way.

HISTORICAL DATA AND POPULATION CYCLES

The question immediately arises whether the logistic equation or its modifications fit data that are available on population changes. The logistic fits reasonably well the recent data on the populations of Europe and North America and the small modifications increase the goodness of fit. These historical data are not, however, of great precision – other than for the nineteenth and twentieth centuries when statistics were collected systematically (Hollingsworth, 1969; Clark, 1967). For earlier centuries they are estimates, some of which are very indirect. Even so these data suggest that at least three cycles of logistic growth have occurred in the population of England since the Norman Conquest. The first consisted of a rapid growth, possibly commencing in about AD 850, well established by the Conquest and petering out around AD 1300. The population was then at a level which was not again to be reached until the eighteenth and early nineteenth century. In the fourteenth century there was a climatic change and the weather conditions for food production became much poorer than before. Famines occurred; the Winchester Account Rolls show these were severe in AD 1315 and 1317; agricultural production fell and so did population. By the time of the Black Death in AD 1348, population had been static and perhaps declining for at least 30 years. The Black Death itself was not responsible for the decline in population growth; this had already occurred before its onset. The plague, however, is thought to have reduced England's population by a further third (Ziegler, 1976). The second cycle in England began after a period of population stability that lasted until about AD 1450. Population then started growing at a rate which reached 0.9% per year, to cease after the middle of the seventeenth century. This was again associated with poor harvests particularly in the north and mortality increased (Grigg, 1980).

The last cycle is the one in which we are placed at the present time and which is now drawing to its close. The number of people in England commenced to rise in the middle of the eighteenth century, was growing at the rate of 1.1% per annum by AD 1801, continued at rates of 1.3 to 1.4% from AD 1840 to 1880 and then declined to a rate of 0.4% by 1939 (Tranter, 1973). Now it is less than 0.1%.

EVIDENCE OF THE PRINCIPLE?

It seems probable that the thirteenth-century population cycle in England and also that of the sixteenth century are examples of the operation of the Malthusian principle and a curtailment of population growth by a reduction in the means of subsistence. Grigg (1980) in his careful analysis indicates that they provide a justification of Malthus. He equally regards the nineteenth-century cycle as not conforming to Malthus' view. In the thirteenth century the positive check of increased mortality was probably paramount; in the sixteenth century both the positive and preventative checks were probably in operation. The above conclusions are couched in terms of uncertainty. This is understandable since the basic information which could lead to firm conclusions is fragmentary and the fragments themselves are of considerable fragility.

The nineteenth-century cycle in England – and indeed the United Kingdom as a whole – seems to have been entirely different in kind. The slowing of population growth was not due to impoverishment and a failure to provide subsistence. This fact and the fact that in the developed world generally, population growth is diminishing, has been taken to show that in a modern world the factors which control population are different from those which Malthus proposed. The problem has been discussed by many including Eversley (1959) to echo the ideas put forward more than a century before by Sadler (see earlier). The consensus view seems to have been that a rise in living standards, the development of 'western civilized habits' and the progress of democratic institutions are sufficient to halt population growth. This same view was expressed by the United Nations Secretariat in 1953. They reported: 'Those who attribute the decline in fertility in Europe to "civilization" as a whole have perhaps most clearly shown this to be true.' Typical of many who wrote about population 30 or 40 years ago is Brody (1945). He wrote: 'In the United States and other western civilized countries, the limitation of population is not caused by plagues or famines, but by more subtle factors at least among middle and upper classes sensitized to their operation . . . we see here the operation of an elegantly delicate mechanism for holding population in check, not involving the cruel ravages of starvation, disease and attack by enemies as we find under natural conditions.'

These arguments are, to say the least, not very convincing. To postulate that the intrinsic rate of natural increase of a population is modified by a mechanism whereby each member of society (or rather those in its higher echelons) senses some subtle effect of the intellectual and societal environment to curtail his and her reproductive potential for the benefit of future generations, hardly ranks as a definitive causal mechanism. There is no doubt that populations in highly developed countries have approached or are approaching a new equilibrium state in which both natality and mortality are low and expectation of life at birth is high, and that this has been accomplished without being accompanied by the misery and vice which Malthus surmised. The causes are unknown.

DEMOGRAPHIC TRANSITION

The ways in which this demographic structure in developed countries has come about is of interest. A plausible description of the phenomenon of change from a societal structure with high birth and death rates to one of low birth and death rates is that usually known as demographic transition. This postulates that a fall in death rate from a high and variable level precedes in time a fall from high and relatively stable values for birth rate. It is the separation in time of these two events that results in the population surge. Demographic transition certainly describes events that occurred in the population of Denmark (Jones, 1981). It does not, however, accord with events in France in which birth and death rates fell synchronously.

From being a description of events, demographic transition has been promoted to a theory, which then implies that it has predictive power. Some postulate that demographic transition will inevitably occur in the less well developed countries of the world, and that a fall in birth rate will take place for no other reason than that it has done so in developed ones. Demographic transition assumes some unknown homeostatic device regulates population; there is no evidence that such a mechanism exists (Bogue, 1969).

In relegating demographic transition from a general theory to a description of events in some countries, we should perhaps reconsider the so-called limit theorems as exemplified by the logistic equation. They too are descriptive rather than analytical – analytical in the sense of ascribing causes or prompting action that would result in populations reaching new equilibria, or indeed the attributes of those equilibria. To fit a logistic equation is to estimate from population data the equilibrium value, *K*; this is not arrived at independently from any consideration of what individuals need. It is simply a number which inserted in the equation leads to close agreement of the *de facto* population at different times with that estimated. The same is true of the intrinsic rate of increase, *r*; this is not a biological estimate of fecundity arrived at independently but simply the parameter of an equation. The equations are wholly descriptive and interpretation of their constants has to be carried out with considerable care. Admittedly these equations describing population growth, whether the logistic, the limit equations, or Malthus' pair, are based on initial assumptions which decide their algebraic form. It is very doubtful, however, whether they are anything other than empirical in nature or have predictive power.

FORECASTING POPULATION

An example of the problem of lack of predictive power relates to the estimates made by the Registrar General of the population of the United Kingdom in 2001. Such estimates are made at intervals and are published annually in the *Annual Abstract of United Kingdom Statistics* from which Figure 3 has been derived. The figure shows that despite the considerable experience and expertise that resides in his office his estimates of population in 2001 have been widely at variance in the last 40 years. Obviously not all the estimates of the future population can be correct! This example of the difficulty of forecasting future population relates to extrapolation from a wealth of information. Other predictions based on simple premises abound in the more popular literature. Sir George Knibbs, statistician to the Government of Australia calculated that if world population were to grow at the rate of 1% per annum for 10,000 years, the progeny of man would have a mass equal to 10^{21} times that of the earth. Similarly, some American authors have stated that with present growth, in the year AD 2330 the population of the world will be such that there will be one person for every square yard of its surface. These arguments are of the nature of a *reductio ad absurdum*; they simply emphasise that the premises on which the extrapolations were

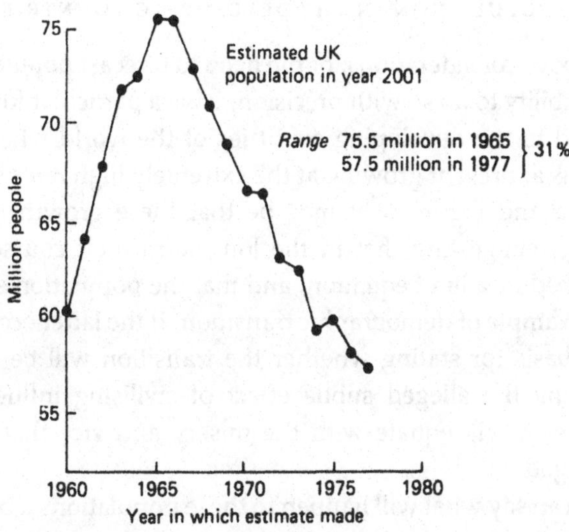

Figure 3 Estimates made in different years by the Registrar General of the United Kingdom's population in the year 2001. This illustrates the considerable difficulties that there are in predicting future population.

based are untenable. The conclusion is unescapable that demography is certainly not an exact science in terms of its ability to predict population and population change with precision.

Yet we desperately need predictions of what the population is likely to be, even if these can only be expressed with reservations or confidence limits. In all countries of the world action has to be taken to cater for the future. Investment policies in relation to education, housing, amenities and social services all depend in scale on estimates of the likely future population. Similarly the planning of utilities, power supplies, construction of reservoirs for drinking water and plant for sewage disposal, and of course the planning of food production, all require decisions to be made, years ahead of the future demand likely to be exerted by the whole population.

POPULATION IN THE DEVELOPING COUNTRIES

The above considerations, of the need to forecast population and the inability to do so with precision, have a particular force when applied to the developing countries of the world where population is at present growing at the extremely high rates shown in Table 2 and Figure 1. It may be that these growth rates will decline, suggesting that in the long term their course will be described by a limit equation, and that the population explosion is an example of demographic transition. If the latter occurs there is no basis for stating whether the transition will be painless, reflecting the alleged subtle effect of civilising influences, or whether it will equate with the misery and vice that Malthus envisaged.

We can say what will happen to these populations if birth rates and death rates in each age class of the population do not change in subsequent years. We cannot, however, justify the assumption that they will not change, or predict if they do change, when and how they will do so. Nevertheless, if we are to make any assessment at all of the magnitude of the problem of the relation between people and the resources of the world, some estimate must be made of the pressure to be exerted solely by the increased number of mankind.

Despite these strictures about the accuracy of demographic prediction, however, certain categorical statements can be made. We can be certain that the population of the developing countries of the world will increase in the immediate future under any tenable and realistic assumptions about the effectiveness of any family limitation policies. These countries have undergone massive population expansion in the past few decades and, as a consequence, the age structures of their populations are heavily biased to include a large proportion – up to 50% in some – of young people below the age of 15. These people will reproduce. Even if all the women in the population suddenly have completed and surviving families of two, the number which would ultimately result in population stability, the population would grow. It would take about 50 years to achieve an equilibrium and during that period the population would increase to one which is 60% greater than that initially. If, more realistically, completed and surviving family size was reduced to two over a period of 25 years, the equilibrium population would be 2.5 times the present one and would take almost 75 years to reach (Keyfitz, 1971; Keyfitz and Flieger, 1971; Ehrlich, Ehrlich and Holdren, 1973). Admittedly these estimates of future population are less than those based on a simple extrapolation of current growth rates; they nevertheless indicate the enormous momentum that population growth in the last 50 years has achieved. It is absolutely certain that the population of the developing countries of the world will increase whatever happens. It can also be concluded that the lower limit to numbers in 50 years' time will be 5,300 millions, or 1.6 times the present one. What the actual number will be, is impossible to forecast. The estimate made by the World Bank (see Haub and Heisler, 1980) suggests that the ultimate size of the population of the developing countries will be 2.6 times the present one, a value which would accord with the premise that the completed and surviving families reached two in a matter of 25 years. Whether this implicit premise is reasonable, one cannot tell.

3
Food and people

THE MEANS OF SUBSISTENCE

In the previous chapter, what Malthus called the means of subsistence was defined indirectly as the capacity of an area to support a population. This indirect definition assumes firstly, that each individual has some requirement for what a land area can provide and secondly, that the aggregate pressure exerted by a population on the land area is the summation of these individual needs. The basic requirements of each individual are for food, shelter, clothing and fuel. One might also add to these a requirement for a social structure to govern the individual's relationship to the community of which he is a part. The above requirements are basic to existence. As societies advance, however, they demand things other than these absolute necessities – consumer goods in our own society are an example – and the question arises whether the minimal list of the needs for survival alone are sufficient in a modern world. In this respect Keynes in his *Essays in Persuasion* (1931) distinguished two classes of human need: 'Those needs which are absolute in the sense that we feel them whatever the situation of our fellow human beings may be, and those which are relative only in that their satisfaction lifts us above, makes us superior to our fellows.' Keynes' distinction obviously applies to a need to satisfy hunger on the one hand, and the desire to own a Rolls Royce on the other. The distinction could perhaps suffice to separate the necessities from the luxuries in a modern world. Whether any such classification arrived at for our own society should then be applied to the world as a whole, or whether each society should define its own is a matter for conjecture. As far as the need for food is concerned, the difficulty of defining the need in absolute terms was well appreciated by James Steuart (1767). He wrote: 'The more rich and luxurious a people are the more delicate they become in the manner of living; if they fed on bread formerly they will now feed on meat; if they fed on meat they will now feed on fowl.' The change in the type of diet with change in living standards can hardly be ascribed to a desire to feel superior. Rather it reflects a desire to eat more acceptable foods once hunger has been assuaged. Steuart was particularly prescient in identifying an increase in living standards with the consumption of better diets. The future strain on the food-producing systems of the world will not be due solely to an increase in the number of consumers. A further component must relate to the aspirations of people to consume these better diets and not simply to exist at a subsistence level.

There is in addition a third component. The calculation of future strain must involve consideration of those people who do not at present receive adequate diets, that is do not receive diets which are sufficient for a normal healthy life and are thus, on any rational basis to be regarded as being below the subsistence level.

THE EXTENT OF MALNUTRITION

There have been many estimates of the number of people in the world who do not receive adequate food. Such estimates are particularly difficult to make for they depend on the setting up of standards of normality from which departures can be assessed. Some examples of these difficulties are given later. It is not surprising that estimates of the numbers of malnourished, or undernourished or hungry people in the world vary considerably – from a tenth to a third of the world's population – for the criteria separating the deprived people from the more fortunate have not been the same for each estimate. Evidence of inadequate nutrition which is unassailable is the presence of disease attributable to nutritional deficiency. Even so, even when there are clear clinical signs of disease, or when there is no doubt that there is nutritional deprivation, determination of what proportion of the population is affected is often not easily done.

NUTRITIONAL DISEASE

To many in the developed countries the extent of overt malnutrition in the developing world comes as a severe shock when they visit the countries concerned. Our nutritional worries in western societies are very different to those encountered in Africa, the east and in South and Central America. We are, rightly or wrongly, concerned about the effects of overconsumption of high quality foods. There is thus concern about the long-term effects of the consumption of saturated fats from dairy produce and meat on the incidence of cardio-vascular disease, the effects of a diminution in the intake of fibrous constituents on gastro-intestinal disease including cancer, the overconsumption of salt and the occurrence of hypertension and, generally, with the effects of a long-continued excessive consumption of a highly palatable and attractive diet in causing obesity. In the poor nations of the world these nutritional problems are not of great concern. Rather, deficiencies of specific nutrients, deficiencies which have long been overcome in richer nations, are commonplace.

Several million people in Bangladesh, particularly in Rangpur, have goitre due to iodine deficiency. The easily recognised syndrome of goitre, cretinism and an associated deaf mutism can affect most peoples in that great sweep of land from Southeast Asia to the Himalayan massive and north into Siberia. In 1966 – over 20 years ago admittedly – in the Everest region of the Nepalese Himalaya 13% of the whole population were cretins and 60% had visible goitre. More recently in the villages of Bangladesh a survey showed that the incidence of goitre was 70%. The disease can readily be prevented by adding iodine as iodide to domestic cooking salt but there is no national programme to undertake this, and, because of suspicion based on illiteracy, there is resistance on the part of people to an acceptance of the medication of their salt supply. There has been no complete survey of the incidence of goitre in the world but conservative estimates place the number of affected people to be in the region of 200 million.

It may be insulting to the reader to imply that he or she has little real conception of the magnitude of this figure of 200 million. Nevertheless, and with apologies, it is useful to attempt to assess its enormity. Assuming that one could count a queue of people at the rate of 100 each minute, in the 24 hours of the day one could count 144,000. To count the 200 million would take somewhat in excess of three years and nine months, counting day and night, night and day.

Pellagra is another nutritional deficiency disease once common in the maize-eating communities of Europe and especially of Italy and of the southern United States. Its cause is a lack in the diet of the B-complex vitamin, niacin, and of the amino acid tryptophan. Maize contains little tryptophan and has much of its niacin present in a bound form. With more varied diets for the peoples in the affected areas of the new world and the old, the disease has virtually disappeared. This is not so on the Deccan in India. There the disease is associated with those whose staple food is *Jowah*, the sorghum *S. vulgar*. This grain is also low in tryptophan and additionally has an imbalance of that amino acid. The disease is not mild; it shows all the classical signs which were attributed to the disease a hundred years ago – dermatitis, diarrhoea and most disturbing of all, dementia. These patients can be seen in the hospitals of Hyderabad where the administration of the vitamin leads to spectacular cures. The people concerned return to their villages, to continue to eat their *Jowah* diets, and return for treatment after a few months. There are no statistics to provide an accurate estimate of incidence.

There are, however, reasonable statistics related to the incidence of nutritional blindness that occurs as a result of vitamin A deficiency. In Indonesia surveys of 30,000 pre-school children showed evidence of active corneal disease with an incidence of 2.7 per 1,000, resulting in 63,000 new cases each year (Sommer, 1982). A recent estimate of the incidence of blindness due to the xerophthalmia which results from vitamin A deficiency in the world as a whole is 250,000 annually (World Health Organisation, 1982; Sommers *et al.*, 1981). If expectation of life of these children was 57 years as it is in the developing world as a whole, then the number of blind could approach 14 millions. In fact many of the affected children suffer from protein-energy malnutrition and the effect of the concomitant vitamin A deficiency is to increase mortality of from 10% to 20% of affected children by almost fourfold (McLaren, 1984). Even when control measures are instituted as in Andhra Pradesh, India, by giving supplementary vitamin A, 5% of children aged 1–5 years had Bitot's spots, the lesion which progresses to corneal xerophthalmia. Despite the programme, vitamin A supplementation reached only 45–50% of the children (Pirie, 1983).

Visitors to India and Bangladesh may well have seen many crippled people. Many of these are the *khesari* eaters who suffer from neurolathyrism. This arises from the presence in the staple winter crop, *khesari* (*Lathyrus sativus*, a type of pea), of a neurotoxin, N oxalylamino-2-aminopropionic acid (Rao, Adiga and Sarma, 1964). After consuming these grains for two to three months an irreversible neural degeneration takes place, particularly in young people. The disease is so common that the hospitals classify those affected as one-stick people, two-stick people or crawlers, but the precise figures for incidence are again not known.

One can multiply the examples of disease occurring on a large scale in the world which is attributable to dietary deficiencies or toxins. The staple cassava diet of many peoples in Africa contains cyanogenic glycosides and these are associated with poor health on a scale that is not known (Osuntokun, 1981). Anaemia, preventable by iron is undoubtedly common in the developing world. In Bangladesh the incidence in children is considerable and this is exacerbated by the high incidence of round worms

(*Ascaris*). Worm burdens in children who are in areas with contaminated water supplies are very high, as evidenced by worm egg counts in the faeces averaging 12,000 per gram. Anthelminthic treatment together with dietary supplements improves the growth of children quite unbelievably (Ahmad, 1981).

One nutritional disease syndrome which has received considerable attention is that usually termed protein–energy malnutrition (Whitehead, 1976). This takes two forms, one a simple wasting called infantile marasmus and the other kwashiorkor, a disease characterised by oedema, an enlarged liver, discoloured hair and extreme apathy. The name for the disease is a word in Ga, a language of West Africa where Cicely Williams the first woman medical officer to the Gold Coast (now Ghana) described the disease. The meaning of this word is 'the disease suffered by the displaced child' (Golden and Jackson, 1984). As Golden (1985) has pointed out there is, as yet, no agreed reason to account for the occurrence of marasmus in some instances and kwashiorkor in others. Both are associated with less than adequate food in the infantile period of growth. Nor is there any agreed estimate of the incidence of this particular type of malnutrition since there is a gradation of clinical signs within populations at risk, from children with unmistakeable clinical signs of wasting to those who are stunted to those who are apparently normal.

DIETARY REQUIREMENTS

Although there is little doubt that clinical disease due to deficiency of nutrients is widespread in the world, there are no precise statistics available to estimate its extent. Still less is there evidence of the extent of malnutrition which, while of insufficient magnitude to give rise to obvious disease, nevertheless causes some impairment of function. One way of assessing the number of people involved is to estimate, either from dietary surveys or from measures of the food supplies entering consumption the people who receive less than the optimal amount of each specific nutrient. This makes the assumptions that the optima can be precisely defined and that downward departures from it lead to an impairment. Neither assumption can be wholly justified.

Man requires in his diet 39 chemically defined nutrients, together with a source of fat and carbohydrate to provide energy, for normal growth and for meeting the demands of pregnancy and lactation. The list of nutrients includes ten essential amino acids, four fat-soluble and eleven water-soluble vitamins, six major mineral elements required in amounts exceeding 250 mg a day and eight minor mineral elements required in lesser amounts. Additionally, the diet should be free of compounds injurious to health. Fluorine, for example, while it may be an essential nutrient for man – there is no firm evidence – is certainly a toxic one. When present in excess it leads to endemic fluorosis which is still present in certain areas of North Africa and in China. Some other toxic constituents of foods have already been mentioned and still others arise from fungal contamination of food commodities.

Human requirements of these nutrients and of energy have been determined, some on an adequate and some on a very limited scale. Where the scale has been adequate in terms of numbers of subjects studied, it is immediately evident that there is a variation in need from individual to individual. It is for this reason that estimates of the mean daily requirement of populations is usually increased by a statistically determined factor which results in a 'recommended daily allowance' which provides sufficient of the nutrient to all but a small proportion of the population. A recommended allowance defined in this way can be regarded as one which if adhered to would ensure that 97% of the population received sufficient. The populations referred to are classes defined by age, sex, and for women, reproductive state, that is whether pregnant or lactating. These statistically defined safety margins are sometimes increased where it is known that requirements are elevated under conditions of stress, disease or prior malnutrition or undernutrition. They are not increased to take into account any variation from time to time or from place to place in the concentrations of nutrients in the foods which make up the diet. The margins of safety simply relate to estimates of the variation of man's physiological needs.

RECOMMENDED DIETARY ALLOWANCES AND PLANNING

The product of number of people and the requirement of nutrients is an estimate of the nutrient needs of the population. These obviously have to be translated into terms of commodities for people do not ingest nutrients, they eat food. Truswell (1983) has stated that recommended dietary allowances can be used to plan food supplies although it is rather doubtful if they are. They can, however, be used to indicate whether a population receives less than what can be regarded as adequate amounts for the majority.

The International Union of Nutritional Sciences has summarised the recommended dietary allowance arrived at by authorities in different countries in the world (IUNS, 1983), and some relevant data are given in Table 3. They show that estimates of the energy requirements of adult man do not vary very much from country to country; lower values from the Southeast Asian countries reflect the lower stature of Phillipinos and Malaysians. Estimates of protein requirements, however, vary widely – by almost twofold – and this large variation is equally evident when protein requirements are expressed relative to the supply of energy-yielding constituents. The differences are little short of absurd. It is inconceivable that a man moving from the United States of America to Czechoslovakia immediately requires a diet nearly twice as rich in protein, and then requires still more if he moves to Bulgaria!

These anomalies with respect to recommended allowances of protein reflect earlier uncertainties about the protein requirements of man, uncertainties which led to unfortunate effects on world food policy in the 1960s and 1970s. The episode is of

Table 3 *The recommended dietary allowances of energy-yielding constituents and of protein for adult men in selected countries*

Country		Energy requirement MJ/day	Protein g/day	g protein/MJ
All countries, mean		11.9	66	5.5
Developed market economies	UK	12.1	72	5.9
	France	11.3	81	7.2
	USA	12.1	56	4.6
Centrally planned economies	Czechoslovakia	12.6	105	8.3
	Bulgaria	12.3	110	8.9
Developing economies	Phillipines	10.8	63	5.8
	Malaysia	10.6	45	4.2

considerable relevance in any attempts to forecast food needs in the future. The events which took place are therefore given in some detail.

THE LEGACY OF MISUNDERSTANDING

In 1965 the joint committee of the FAO and the World Health Organisation (WHO), charged with estimating the protein requirement of man, concluded that the 'safe' amount of protein to be provided for the populations of the world was 0.71 g per kg body weight. This was a minimal need for high quality protein such as that of egg, and for proteins of lower nutritive worth actual requirements were to be increased according to the nutritive value as measured in laboratory trials with rats. It was assumed that this estimate of need for protein of particular quality together with estimates of the amounts of protein consumed would define the number of people who received insufficient and hence the amount of protein necessary to be produced on a world scale to make good the deficiency. This approach, which is exactly the same as that already briefly discussed, seems eminently sensible. The results were frightening: whole countries apparently had populations which received less than an optimal amount of protein. The United Nations was so concerned that it established an entirely new agency, The Protein Advisory Group, to deal with what was regarded as a very serious nutritional crisis. A document was indeed published under the title 'International action to avert the impending protein crisis', urging all governments to increase protein supplies using modern fermentation technologies to produce single cell protein as well as by diverting land to the production of protein-rich legumes and livestock. The world food problem was immediately identified as a protein supply problem, and because of the reputation of the United Nations organisation, this view was accepted by governments and ordinary people alike.

It was Donald McLaren, then working at the American University of Beirut, who finally brought better understanding to bear in a paper in 1974 which he entitled 'The great protein fiasco', pointing out that the emphasis given to the role of protein in human undernutrition was wrong. There was no global protein gap, crisis or problem but rather shortages of energy-yielding food. Sukhatme (1971) had earlier uncovered the faulty statistical and biological logic in the committee's pronouncement. So too had Clark and Turner (1973) who wrote: 'Protein deficiency is primarily a result of low calorie intake and thus the body's ability to use what protein is consumed. These conclusions are quite the opposite of these of Scrimshaw and his coworkers. They have thought that protein is the primary limiting factor. The United Nations report "International action to avert the impending protein crisis" and its call to nations to deal explicitly with the protein problem, recommending the production of protein foods using non-agricultural techniques are based on Scrimshaw's work. The conclusions arrived at here lead to different and indeed simpler solutions.' Sukhatme in his paper had been even more direct. He said: 'People can have enough and more of the protein they need from the cereal/pulse diet they normally consume if only they can eat enough to satisfy their energy demands.'

Obviously there were rejoinders from those who believed that protein was the major deficit in human diets. Scrimshaw (1977) thus stated: 'The problem from a global perspective has been assessed by the Advisory Group of the UN which has repeatedly tried to explain that the protein gap is not a lack of overall supplies but rather a gap between what is consumed by the affluent compared with the poorest most vulnerable segments of the population. It is a gap that will not be closed by the simple expedient of improving production.' If this was the reason for establishing the group, firstly it does not explain its insistence on greater production, and secondly it is not clear on what basis the dietary adequacy of the poor was assessed.

The later reports of nutritional advisers to FAO and WHO revised the estimates of protein need downwards by from 20 to 25%. By this device alone tens if not hundreds of millions of people were reclassified from being nutritionally deprived to being adequately fed with respect to protein. The amounts of protein involved were enormous. The 1965 estimates were minimally 10 g per person per day higher than those later suggested. For poor diets the difference was greater than 10 g. A difference in mean minimal need of the individual of 10 g implies a need to produce about 15 million tons of first class protein annually for the world as a whole – a prodigous quantity. At the present time many advisors think that the current recommendations are possibly slightly low. This supposition, if correct, suggests that there are people who although receiving sufficient protein by international standards are in fact receiving less than the desirable amount.

This episode illustrates one aspect of the problem of interpreting physiological measurements made on human subjects in terms of national food policies or indeed international ones. The physiological measurements may not be sufficiently precise or widely enough based to warrant overall statements, particularly when the variation within a small number of subjects is extrapolated to vast numbers of people in terms of a margin of safety. The example of protein is not the only one; the same applies to estimates of the requirement for calcium. The Walkers (1981), for example, have pointed out that in many developing countries it is virtually impossible to meet the recommended intakes of both protein and calcium during pregnancy and lactation from the habitual diet. Yet these women lactate successfully and for prolonged periods when receiving about a quarter of the recommended daily allowance of 1,200 mg calcium. This is so even when they have successive pregnancies at relatively short intervals. Careful studies show that the bones of these women show no signs of the mineral depletion which would be expected were they deficient in calcium (Walker, Richardson and Walker, 1972). Clearly these women can get by with a quarter of the recommended allowance, which suggests either that the estimates of daily requirement are wrong or that, over long periods of time, people can adapt to lower than so-called normal intakes.

Returning to the variation in the recommended daily allowances of protein evident in Table 3 it appears that some is due to whether or not the countries concerned took cognisance of the 1965 or the 1973 pronouncements or even the earlier ones made by the FAO in 1957. There has always been a wide difference of opinion about whether the minimal requirement of man for protein is synonymous with the optimal one. It may well be that the persistence of older estimates of protein requirements which were derived simply from what healthy people in western societies habitually consumed is an indication of a caution on the part of the authorities responsible for the recommendations and a belief that provision of more protein than a minimal amount in some way confers an advantage.

NUTRITIONAL ADAPTATION

The example of the possibility of an accommodation of metabolism to a lowered dietary supply of a nutrient applied to calcium. Such accommodation also probably applies to certain other mineral elements, including phosphorus and iron. It has, however, a deeper implication when applied to the requirement for the energy-yielding constituents of food. Some account of responses to energy undernutrition is necessary to reveal this implication.

If man is given a diet containing less energy-yielding constituents than is normally consumed and on which weight is maintained, or growth is quite satisfactory, two things can happen. A reduction in the amount of energy expended in work or other bodily activity can occur to ensure that a balance between the intake and expenditure of energy is maintained. This reduction in activity is usually insufficient and the fat and protein of the body are oxidised to supply the deficit, with a corresponding loss of body weight and, for a child, a reduced rate of growth. In the long term a new balance is established between intake and expenditure at a lowered body weight, a somewhat reduced vital activity as measured by the basal metabolic rate and, with children, a lowered rate of gain in body weight. These changes can be regarded as the devices used by the body to preserve life in the face of adversity.

It is immediately pertinent to ask whether the small stature of some peoples in the developing countries of the world is indeed due to long-continued subsistence on diets containing low amounts of energy. If this is so then dietary standards based on the body weights of these people, their measured metabolic rates and their habitual activity patterns cannot be regarded as optimal in the wider sense of that term. The recommended allowances given in Table 3 for Malaysians and Phillipinos may well reflect, not their genetic constitution but legacies of undernutrition over generations.

There is certainly evidence to suggest that nurture and not nature is the reason for small stature. The secular changes in the height of children in the United Kingdom since the middle nineteenth century has certainly coincided with an increase in the nutritional status of the whole population, and the same is true of the more recent increase in child stature in Japan. Earlier, the Japanese immigrants into North America were after a generation or two found to be larger than their erstwhile compatriots. The Hong Kong Chinese are now allowed to visit the People's Republic of China and one notices them, not because of their transistor radios and less conservative dress, but because they are distinctly taller and somewhat broader than the native Han people.

Additionally, there is some evidence to show that at the same body weight the basal metabolic rates of Indians is less than that of Europeans (Schofield, 1985), and the analysis of older data which suggested that basal metabolic rate was lower in hot than in cold countries could well reflect the same thing, for most of the less well developed countries are in what is usually termed 'the South' (Quenouille *et al.*, 1951). Lastly the apparent lethargy of some peoples in the warmer and less well developed countries may not simply be innate or a reaction to the climate but evidence of an adjustment to a long-continued nutritional deprivation.

These considerations suggest that present dietary recommendations for the inhabitants of the less well developed countries may not be optimal in the long term. Gopalan, an Indian nutritionist in an article (1983) with the somewhat provocative title '"Small is healthy", for the poor, not for the rich', argues that the majority of India's children are malnourished in some degree. There is intense debate on what indeed should be the nutritional standards applied in the poorer countries both to assess the extent of what may be called 'hidden undernourishment' and to plan food production for the future (see Blaxter and Waterlow, 1985; Pollitt and Amante, 1984).

CRUDE ESTIMATES OF HUNGER

Although there are uncertainties attached to estimates of what people require in terms of the nutrients and energy supplied by their diets, there is little doubt that in many, but not all, developing countries intakes are below even minimal estimates of requirement. This is shown by the latest estimates made by the

FAO (1983) of the food supply in individual countries. In Table 4 four of the poorest countries in Asia and in Africa are compared with four European countries. The lower intakes in poor Asian and African countries than in Europe could be due to smaller stature of the peoples of those countries, or as we have seen the very reverse. The final rows of the table show that people in the poor Asian and African countries receive about 56% of the energy and 50% of the protein which Europeans receive. The ratio of protein to energy in their food supply is not so greatly different; those in these poorer countries simply receive less food qua food. A comparison of the amounts supplied in these selected Asian and African countries with the American recommended daily allowances is reasonable. The United States adhered to the 1973 recommendations of the United Nations with respect to protein and the allowance is thus not enhanced by the faulty assessment of protein need discussed earlier. Not one of the poorer countries in Table 4 receives anything approaching the recommended allowance for energy of the United States and only one does so with respect to protein. Again differences in stature and habits may be responsible for this failure to reach the standards of the United States. Equally the differences in stature could reflect that they have not done so for generations. Whatever way the data are regarded they suggest that in these countries people are indeed hungry.

FUTURE FOOD NEEDS

The same uncertainties surrounding estimates of the nutrient needs of populations as a yardstick for assessing current sub-optimal nutrition apply to their use in estimating future needs for nutrients and hence for food commodities. An alternative approach is to assess future food needs on an economic basis by estimating how far the income of the world's population will augment. Then with estimates of the income elasticity of demand for food, demand in terms of commodities can be derived. These income elasticities of demand are the proportional changes in the

Table 4 *The food supply* in terms of energy (MJ per person per day) and of protein (g per person per day) in selected countries*

Group	Country	Food supply/day		
		Energy (MJ)	Protein (g)	Protein/Energy g/MJ
Poorest Asian countries	Bangladesh	7.5	36.3	4.9
	India	8.4	48.2	5.7
	Kampuchea	7.4	40.1	5.4
	Laos	7.7	47.7	6.2
Poorest African countries	Ethiopia	7.3	57.5	7.9
	Ghana	8.4	36.6	4.4
	Zambia	8.3	52.3	6.3
	Tanzania	8.5	43.8	5.2
European countries	Denmark	14.0	87.4	6.2
	France	14.3	97.9	6.8
	Hungary	14.9	95.7	6.4
	UK	13.7	87.1	6.4
Mean unweighted values Europe = 100				
Europe		100	100	100
Poorest Asian		55	47	86
Poorest African		57	52	91

**Note:* This is the *supply* of food other than fish, not the amounts consumed.

quantity purchased divided by the proportional change in income, price being constant. They vary with the level of income and with the socio-economic status of the people. Obviously subdivisions can be made; individual countries or indeed identifiable groups within countries can be considered separately to arrive at estimates of likely future demand by an augmented population, and one would hope, one with a greater income. Such a calculation of likely future food demand is also beset with

Table 5 *Growth rates (% per annum) of population and food supply in certain regions of the world*

Region	1952–60 Population	1952–60 Food supply	1961–70 Population	1961–70 Food supply	1971–80 Population	1971–80 Food supply
Developed countries	1.3	3.2	1.1	2.6	0.8	1.9
Africa	2.2	2.8	2.5	2.6	2.9	1.8
Latin America	2.8	3.2	2.9	3.5	2.7	3.9
Asia	2.6	3.4	2.2	2.7	2.0	3.2
			Per capita food supply			
Developed countries	+1.9		+1.5		+1.1	
Africa	+0.6		+0.1		−1.1	
Latin America	+0.4		+0.6		+1.1	
Asia	+1.4		+0.5		+1.2	

uncertainties. One is related to future population size, another to future income and a third to likely elasticities in some hypothetical distribution of income in the population. The estimate is likely to be as imprecise as the product, future population times nutrient need and the conversion factor which transforms estimates of nutrients needed to one in terms of commodities. In any event it does not seem reasonable to link future food requirements to purely economic assessments. Surely some consideration has to be given to the amelioration of hunger, malnutrition and undernutrition as an end in itself. Aspects of other economic arguments relating to food and people are deferred until later.

If neither a nutritional approach nor an economic one are satisfactory in predicting future need, one can resort to using the past as an indicator of the magnitude of likely future problems. Table 5 compares the growth rates of population and of their food supply in successive decades for major regions of the world. In the developed world and in Asia and Latin America food production has grown faster than has population, with an increase in the average amount of food available per capita. In Africa, however, per capita food production hardly changed in the 1960s and in the last decade has become negative. Africa is losing the battle if not the long-term war against sub-optimal nutrition of its peoples.

4

Nutrients and commodities

THE MAGNITUDE OF THE TASK

In the two previous chapters emphasis was given to the limitations of both the demographic and nutritional components of the product, likely future number of people in the world times likely future food requirement of the average person. Even so, estimates of both components are necessary to assess the magnitude of the overall problems that beset mankind. One can commence with the population projections made by the World Bank (1984).

The World Bank, drawing on the United Nations' data on population and vital statistics, has undertaken, country by country, an analysis of trends in the basic parameters that determine population size. It has made assumptions about future mortality and future fertility, taking into account the likely success of family planning programmes, to arrive at estimates of the year in which fertility would reach a replacement level. Then demographic methods are employed, which take into account the changing age structure of the population, to provide estimates of the size of the population at equilibrium and the course which population growth will take. It should be noted that the projections assume that each and every country will eventually reduce fertility to a level which results in replacement and no more; it states that a limit to population is inevitable without ascribing any cause.

Table 6 summarises the calculations by economic region of the world and Table 7 gives results for individual countries. For the world as a whole, the estimate suggests that in the short time to the year 2000 there will be 33% more people to be fed or an extra

1,500 million people. In the developed areas of the world the increase will be only about 9%; in the less well developed ones in excess of 40%. The ultimate size of the world's population is estimated to be 2.4 times the present one. The data for individual countries in Table 7 reflect the assumptions that the World Bank made; thus China's programmes for population limitation are assumed to be effective, and the absence of early change in fertility in the estimates for Bangladesh and Nigeria show their appreciation of the difficulties of curtailing family size in those countries.

FOOD EQUITY

These population estimates by the World Bank are probably optimistic in the long term – we cannot tell – but in the shorter term until the year 2000 are probably not grossly in error. If the average amount of food consumed by the individual does not change then the increase in food production required to be achieved by the year 2000 would be 33%. It can be argued that the average amount of food consumed in 1982 is an adequate measure of human need; after all it was sufficient to allow an increase in the world's population to take place. Reproduction however, persists in the face of deprivation and an average assumes an equity where none exists. Such an average discounts the extent of current and overt malnutrition in some and nutritional affluence in others, as discussed in the previous chapter.

The argument that the total food requirement in the year 2000 can be estimated from population increase alone leads to another. It has been suggested that there is at present sufficient food in the world to provide for all were it but equitably distributed. This subsidiary argument is plausible; it may even be true. It ignores, however, the aspiration of people everywhere for what may be called for simplicity 'better diets', that is for diets which are those of the present affluent. An estimate of the amount of food required in the future could well be based on some concept of equity; however, it has to be accepted that such

Table 6 *Estimates made by the World Bank (1984) of the future population of different economic regions of the world*

Type of economy	Population in 1982 (millions)	Projected population in 2000 (millions)	Theoretical assumed maximum population (millions)
Low income (including China and India)	2,267	3,097	5,863
Middle income (including Indonesia and Brazil)	1,163	1,741	3,729
Oil exporters (including Saudi Arabia)	17	33	96
Industrial market (including Europe and USA)	723	780	828
Eastern European (including USSR)	384	431	523
All	4,554	6,082	11,039
Relative: 1982 = 1.0	1.0	1.33	2.42

an equity does not imply constancy over time because human wants as well as basic needs enter into the calculations.

The most basic of all dietary needs is that for the energy-yielding constituents of food. It seems reasonable to state as an immediate goal that those in the developing countries of the world should receive the same number of megajoules (or calories, one Mcal being equivalent to 4.18 MJ) as those in the developed ones. In the developed countries the supply of food measured in this way is approximately 14 MJ or 3,400 kcal. That in the low-income economies of Table 6 is only 9.3 MJ or 2,200 kcal. Weighting estimates of the energy supplied by food in different countries by their populations leads to a present value for the average amount of energy supplied by food of 10.9 MJ or 2,600 kcal. On this basis the immediate need is to

Table 7 *Estimates made by the World Bank (1984) of the future population of some individual countries*

Country	Population in 1982 (millions)	Projected population in 2000 (millions)	Theoretical assumed maximum population (millions)	Year in which the net reproduction rate decreased to equal 1.0
Bangladesh	93	157	454	2035
India	717	994	1,707	2010
Tanzania	20	36	117	2030
China	1,008	1,196	1,461	2000
Ghana	12	24	83	2030
Indonesia	153	212	370	2010
Nigeria	91	169	618	2035
Brazil	127	181	304	2010
UK	56	57	59	2010
Japan	118	128	128	2010
USA	232	259	292	2010
USSR	270	306	377	2000

increase the food supply per capita by almost a third. The immediate future requirement of food expressed in terms of energy for the world's population would thus seem to be compounded of two terms of equal magnitude, one representing population growth, the other provision of an equitable supply of food per person. The product of these implies that the problem in the period up to the year 2000 is to increase the supply of food by about 75% of its current level. This estimate is very similar to that arrived at by the Food and Agriculture Organisation in their analysis in 1981.

To the farmers within the European Economic Community the idea that there is a need to increase food production by 75% in the short space until the year 2000 or to double it in the next quarter of a century must seem bizarre, when their essentially parochial problem is one of surplus agricultural production. It must seem so too to farmers in the United States and Canada, and in Australia and New Zealand. The problem is clearly one which relates to the world other than Europe or North America or Oceania. These developed regions cannot, however, ignore the problem, nor would many in the countries concerned wish to do so.

FOOD AND COMMODITIES

The data used to estimate the increase necessary in food energy for each individual were in terms of supply, not in terms of amounts consumed. These supplies are usually expressed as items of commerce – grain, carcases of animals, unprocessed roots etc. Grain is normally milled, not all the carcase of an animal is eaten (though in Accra grass-cutter soup is made from the whole animal including its digestive tract contents and skin!), and vegetable preparation involves waste. Furthermore, not all foods or commodities require similar resources to produce them. The energy provided by what is consumed, the quantities of produce required to meet this dietary need and the resources necessary to grow and harvest the produce, demand separate consideration.

Food production depends on the fundamental resource of land. Some food is produced from the oceans and fish may loom large in the diets of some people, but in the world as a whole, fish accounts for only 1% of the total energy consumed. Land, and particularly cropped land as distinct from range land, is the major source of food. The output from cropped land is the product of its area, the frequency with which it is cropped and the yield of the crop at harvest. Cropping frequency can sometimes be three crops per year in wet rice-growing areas with adequate water but is more commonly two. In most temperate regions cropping frequency is one and in many tropical areas where there is shifting cultivation and land is allowed to regenerate after a short cycle of cropping, frequency is considerably less than one. This crop output is termed primary production. If animals depend on this cropped land then the output of food is the product of crop output and the efficiency of the animals in converting the crop to products edible by man. These efficiencies are not high; under best conditions they are about 10% for meat production and about 20% for milk production (Holmes, 1977). Efficiencies are somewhat complex figures for not only do they include the inevitable losses that are involved in converting feed to meat or milk by the individual animal, but they also include the cost of maintaining the breeding flocks and herds and replacing them as they are reduced by old age or disease. Additionally any mortality of young growing livestock involves the expenditure of feed with no return, thus reducing still further the overall efficiency of the conversion process for the herd as a whole. The more primitive the husbandry, the poorer the methods for control of disease and parasitism, the lower the efficiency of the conversion and the greater the land resource needed to produce unit output.

GRAIN EQUIVALENTS

A concept, first put forward by Buck (1937) in relation to China and developed by Clark and Haswell (1967), shows that animal agriculture based on potentially croppable land only emerges when food production exceeds a subsistence level. In the approach employed, food production is expressed in terms of grain output per person, converting root and leaf vegetables to grain by multiplying their fresh weight by five. A man who produces 260 kg grain each year or 700 g per day – an amount which, when losses in preparation are taken into account, provides a mere 10 MJ of dietary energy daily – is at the absolute minimal level for subsistence. Improvements in his output up to 500 kg leads to barter or sale of part of the crop to provide other essentials for existence. Above that level a draught animal can be kept, which exists for the most part on straws and other vegetable wastes. Sustained production equivalent to more than 750 kg grain each year enables croppable land to be devoted

Table 8 *The grain equivalent output of UK agriculture*

Commodity	Output (million tons)	Factor to convert to grain	Grain equivalent (million tons)
Wheat milled	2.9		
Barley malted	3.7		
Sugar	1.2	1.0	12.2
Legume and rape-seed	0.4		
Export grains	4.0		
Potatoes	7.1	0.15	1.5
Vegetables	2.7		
Ruminant meat	1.48	10	
Pig meat	0.89	6.7	24.5
Poultry meat	0.75	5.0	
Eggs	0.66	5.0	3.3
Milk (million litres)	15.2	0.9	13.7
Total			55.2

Grain equivalent per capita $\frac{55.2 \times 10^6}{56 \times 10^6} \approx 1000$ kg

Source: Annual Abstract of Statistics 1982 and efficiency calculations derived from Holmes (1977)

solely to supporting livestock. An agricultural economy which is based on diversion of potentially croppable land to provision of animal feed means that land is present in excess of immediate need. To place these figures in perspective the output of the United Kingdom can be considered in terms of grain equivalent. This has been done in Table 8 and shows how far our agricultural production for 56 million people is removed from the subsistence level. We can clearly afford to devote resources to the support of a livestock economy, despite the fact that to do so entails using foreign exchange to purchase, mainly in American markets, the large amounts of soya products needed to support it.

Livestock are not solely an indication that food production has reached levels at which animal products can be afforded; animals are kept for other reasons. Firstly, the by-products of agriculture which man cannot eat can be consumed by stock to produce food for him. Obvious examples are the use of rice and other straws for the support of cattle and buffalo, the use of vegetable waste in large parts of the Far East for the maintenance of pigs and fresh water fish, the use of the outer seed coats of cereal grains for cattle and the use of the residues of crushing olive, ground nut, soya, palm and other products by all classes of stock. These various seed by-products account for about a quarter of the feed given to livestock, apart from any forage they receive. Secondly, and more important, there are vast tracts of land that, because of their topography, elevation or lack of access, cannot be cultivated to produce crops. In the United Kingdom obvious examples are the hills of Scotland, Wales and northern England where sheep represent a way of obtaining food from a very poor resource. Grazing ruminant livestock is the only way in which much of the semi-arid and arid lands can be made to provide a harvest of food. The husbandry is extensive for the amount of herbage available is both sparse and scant. A third reason is that livestock represent wealth, particularly to nomadic peoples. Livestock are used as part of bride price in some parts of Africa and possession of livestock confers some social advantage.

Undoubtedly, the major reason why animals are kept is to provide draught for farming, for industry and for transport. 20% of the world's population is wholly dependent on cattle, buffalo, horses, asses, mules and camels as sources of tractive power. Some may be employed for but a few days each year at the peak times of heavy cultivation of the paddy fields, when the small amount of gain they had made when eking out an existence on rice straw is soon lost. These animals also provide some food to the peoples concerned.

STAPLE CROPS

If one calculates the total production of primary crops in terms of the energy they could provide if consumed by people, then over 70% of the world's primary production is accounted for by cereals. Root crops such as potatoes, sweet potatoes, cassava, and yams account for about 10%, fruits and vegetables about 8%, sugar from beet or cane approximately 5% and the remaining 7–8% consists of pulses and oil seeds. Of the cereals, wheat and rice predominate. When, however, the amounts of these commodities which enter human consumption are considered using the same measure, it is immediately apparent that these are considerably less than those produced. Only about 65% of the rice produced enters the world supply of food, about 50% of the wheat and less than 20% of the maize and barley. This reflects the use of these grains by livestock and attrition as a result of storage pests and diseases.

Miller (1980) has calculated that the primary output of crops in the world can be apportioned to direct consumption and to indirect consumption, that is to animal products. From food balance sheets the amounts of food, including food of animal origin, moving into human consumption can be expressed in terms of energy. Food production can be computed in the same terms. The results of his calculation are given in Table 9. They indicate that half the primary production is given to livestock which then contribute less than a fifth of the food consumed by man. The calculation neglects the forage which is grown on cultivated land and the contribution made by natural grazings. This is why the efficiency of the conversion of primary human food to secondary animal products is so much higher than the efficiencies given earlier. The calculation nevertheless indicates the magnitude of the diversion of crops potentially edible by man to the support of livestock.

THE LIVESTOCK-VERSUS-CROPS ARGUMENT

A persuasive argument which in part relates to the view that food in the world is plentiful if only it could be rationally and fairly distributed, is that the potential human food – and particularly the grain that is fed to livestock – could be used to improve the nutritional lot of vast numbers who do not have

Table 9 *Miller's (1979) calculation of the disposition of human food from primary crop production (values expressed as MJ per person per day in the world)*

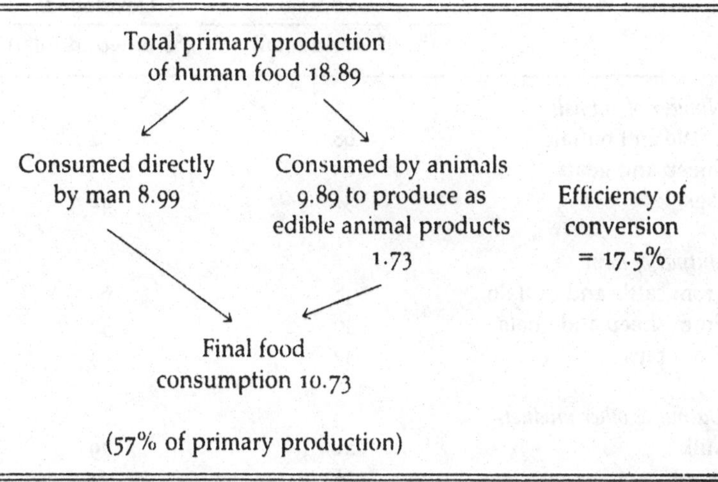

sufficient to eat. The argument is usually illustrated by reference to the large amounts of maize grain given to cattle, pigs and poultry in the United States of America in particular and in the developed world in general. The concept that animal agricultures only develop on cropped land when the produce of that land is in excess of a basic need, has already been given; the animal–crop argument is thus really about a lack of equity in the availability of land of high agricultural potential and in the means to realise that potential. As poorer countries move into cereal surplus it has been the experience that poultry industries arise to deal with surplus grain. Poultry are an excellent choice of animal. Firstly, they produce eggs and meat which are acceptable to virtually all ethnic and religious groups. Secondly, the industries can be expanded and contracted very quickly so to accommodate to year-by-year variation in the surplus grain and, thirdly, the investment required is relatively small.

A perspective on the argument that livestock are superfluous is perhaps given by their number and their distribution. In the

Table 10 *The relative numbers and productivity of livestock in the developed and developing countries of the world (FAO, 1983)*

	Developing (% of world total)	Developed (% of world total)
Number of animals		
Cattle and buffalo	68	32
Sheep and goats	65	35
Pigs	58	42
Output of meat		
From cattle and buffalo	34	66
From sheep and goats	50	50
From pigs	37	63
Output of other products		
Milk	21	79
Wool	26	74

world as a whole, every family of four, whether rural or urban, is on a statistical basis accompanied by 1.3 cattle or buffalo, 1.6 pigs, 0.7 sheep and 6 poultry! Their distribution in the world is given in Table 10 together with estimates of their productivity. The numbers of livestock in the developing countries are greater than in the developed ones but their productivity is far less. It is true that large amounts of grain are fed to stock in the developed world; the productivity of stock in the developing world could equally be increased were there a surplus of grain to feed to them. Again the argument comes back to the basic lack of equity in primary production per capita as between the developed and developing regions.

5
Physical resources

THE RESOURCES FOR FOOD PRODUCTION

Land has already been mentioned as the basic resource on which food production depends. Land must have a supply of water and an equitable temperature as well as an intrinsic fertility if it is to produce a crop. A second resource is the labour of man, a resource which should include the ingenuity, inventiveness and skill of those who breed new crop plants or devise new husbandry techniques, as well as of those who till the fields and tend the stock. In many subsistence societies, land and labour are the sole resources, and this is true of many communities within the developing world. In more advanced agricultures there is a third resource which can be termed the industrial or ex-farm resource. This resource includes equipment and machinery, fuel and power applied in farm operations, fertilisers, agrochemicals for pest, disease and weed control, and transport. These inputs into farming are relatively new and have the effect of expanding the limits of agriculture beyond the immediate fields of the farmer's endeavours. In Britain such an enlargement began with the emergence of wrights and smiths as people separate from the farm proper, making equipment for farm use. It continued with the establishment of machinery manufacturers, and, with the discovery of artificial fertilisers and chemical means of augmenting crop yield and animal production, the process has accelerated further. A convenient collective term for these resources which are external to the farm is 'support energy' because all the varied products brought to the farm involve the expenditure of energy resources, mostly at present from fossil sources, to fabricate them (Odum, 1971). Nevertheless, some of the ex-farm resources, while embraced by the collective term, need separate consideration since they draw on other world resources. Examples are the supply of phosphate rock and to a lesser extent potassic deposits for use as fertiliser.

All three of these resources (land, labour and support energy) have the dimension of power, that is energy per unit time. This is obvious with respect to labour and support energy for the one is usually termed manpower and the other is usually expressed as the expenditure of fossil fuel or its equivalent per year. Land also represents power – not in its sense of dominion but in terms of physics. Every square metre of land receives incoming solar radiation and this is the power which every living creature ultimately taps. An acre of land is an acre of energy in terms of solar radiation.

These three resources, land, labour and support energy are interrelated. Obviously support energy can substitute for manpower, since work done by man can be done by machine. It can also substitute for land if, for example a tractor substitutes for both a man and his pair of horses, because the horses required land for their subsistence. It has been the experience of countries with highly sophisticated agricultures, however, that the application of support power goes far beyond a simple substitution. Increased power, through mechanisation, increased use of fertilisers and improved control of weeds, pests and diseases, leads to increased crop yield, that is to an increase in the proportion of incoming solar radiation which is captured as food by man.

While the three resources are complexly interrelated, a consideration of manpower is given in a separate chapter. The reason is that in many of the developing countries the labour force consists of over three quarters of the whole population. There is no separation of the people who produce food from those who need it. Here the physical rather than the human resources on which food production depends are examined, but the interrelations of the three factors in production must be kept in mind.

Table 11 *Increases in wheat production in major growing areas before and after the second world war and the relative importance of increase in area cropped and in yield per unit area*

Period	Region or country	Total increase in output (%)	Increase in area cropped (%)	Increase in yield per unit area (%)
1909–13 to 1935–39	Australia	88	71	10
	USA	13	24	−9
	Danube basin	88	76	7
1969–71 to 1981	N. America	86	51	24
	UK	104	52	34
	India	75	30	34
	China	92	15	67

WORLD CEREAL OUTPUT

Since cereals account for more than 70% of the crops grown for food and constitute 50% of the food consumed by the world's people, some account of the increase that has taken place in its production is necessary. Table 11 gives some pre-1939 results from major wheat-growing areas of the world and the increases in production that have accrued in the last decade in certain countries. The data show that the increase in wheat production before the war was largely due to an increase in the area planted to the crop, increases in yield per unit area being relatively small or, as in the United States, negative. The table shows that in the last decade, increases in yield per hectare have been considerable. Even so, with the exception of China, the increased output has again largely been due to an increase in the acreage planted. In the world as a whole in the twenty years from 1950 to 1970, wheat production rose by 78%. In the same period the acreage planted increased by 24% and yield per hectare by 43%. During the last decade (1972–82) the increase in wheat production in the world as a whole has been 38%, the area increase being 11% and the yield increase 24%.

Much of the increase in the acreage planted with wheat has been at the expense of acreages planted with other crops. Wheat, which is a relatively new crop in Bangladesh, is, for example, replacing the *khesari* crop, while in northern Europe oats and to a lesser extent rye are being replaced by wheat and barley. Even so, new land has been brought into cultivation.

CHANGES IN LAND USE

Table 12 shows the change in the disposition of land in the decade ending in 1980. Pasture land in the table includes some scrub land and the category 'other land' includes arctic and hot deserts, inhospitable mountains and land used for urban and industrial purposes. In the short space of ten years cropped land has increased in the developing world by 36 million hectares, permanent crops being included. The area of forested land has decreased by more than double this amount and there has been an increase in other land by an amount similar to the increase in the cropped acreage. Part of the latter increase relates to desertification, where population pressure on the land resource has been of major importance. The sequence of events in the Sahel, for example, shows that in the famine of 1968 to 1973, in which a quarter of a million people died, a cycle of drought and degradation of the limited carrying capacity of the land took place through the overgrazing of livestock. Cultivation was extended into fragile areas, livestock were moved into ones which could not support them even if rainfall had been average. It was not. Drought resulted in disaster. The same sequence of events is currently being repeated, aggravated of course by war.

Over half the forested area which has gone in the developing world – 43 million hectares – is in Latin America, where cropped land has only increased by 17 million hectares. A third of the world's vanished forests – 24 million hectares – is in Africa, where cropped land has only increased by 11 million hectares.

Table 12 *Changes in land use in the world in the ten years 1970–1980 (areas in million hectares)*

	Developed world		Developing world	
	Area in 1970	Change in 10 years	Area in 1970	Change in 10 years
Land area	5,484		7,591	
Arable area	650	−3	678	+30
Permanent crops	23	0	64	+6
Pasture	1,279	−8	1,842	−3
Forest	1,861	−26	2,348	−76
Other land	1,671	+37	2,647	+44

To provide a perspective on these enormous acreages a comparison can be made with the United Kingdom. The total area of the United Kingdom is 24 million hectares and our arable land amounts to 7 million hectares. The current rate of reduction in the forested area of the world (FAO, 1982) is 11.3 million hectares per annum; the area being felled in two years is thus nearly equivalent to the area of the UK.

The world statistics suggest that the reason for this felling is not to create new land for cropping. Rather, it is to produce timber for sale to generate foreign exchange. There is a further factor. It has been estimated (Poore, 1983) that a quarter of the world's population depends on forests as a source of fuel wood and at the present time it appears that they are meeting their needs by using wood at a faster rate than it is being replaced. This accelerates the erosion of the forest area. Shifting cultivation in which forest is cut, burned and crops planted before the land is allowed to fall back into forest, while it increases the land under cultivation, leads, as a result of population pressure, to its degradation. Tropical soils are difficult to manage and as the length of the fallow period shortens so does crop yield fall. The length of the bush fallow period has decreased in Sierra Leone by over two years in a decade and it is estimated that its yield under crops has fallen in proportion. The carrying capacity of the land under this system is estimated to be 25 people per square kilometre; the population is now 38 per square kilometre, with consequent further pressure on the resource.

The increase in the category 'other land' deserves comment with respect to its increase in the developed countries. From an analysis by OECD (1979) it appears that in the developed countries alone there is a loss of a third of a million hectares of agricultural land each year to urban spread. In Japan the loss from 1960 to 1970 was estimated to be 7.3% of its total agricultural area. The same process is taking place in the developing world as urbanisation proceeds. Thus in Egypt it has been calculated that as fast as additional areas are irrigated by the Asswan High Dam, old lands are being taken out of cultivation for urban, road and industrial development. The land taken for urban use always seems to be the land which has been cultivated the longest and is usually the better land. This is understandable. The settlements made by our forebears were founded in proximity to land which was easily worked and reasonably fertile. Concentrations of people and of animals led to improvement of the soil by incorporation of their excreta. These settlements expanded to become towns and then cities by peripheral expansion, thus taking the better land. This is very evident in Canada. The best soils in Canada are found in the Ontario Peninsula and to a lesser extent in the Fraser Valley. Soils there are far superior to those of the Canadian Shield, and it is on these better soils that the greatest erosion by urban and industrial development has taken place.

These considerations show that care has to be taken in the interpretation of such beguilingly simple statistics as those in Table 12. The crude data do not illustrate the flux of land. They do not show that good land is being removed from the stock of agricultural land by change to urban use, or that the poorer and climatically vulnerable farming land can degenerate into semi-desert, or that forest land, denuded by felling and the harvesting of fuel wood, can then contribute neither to the forest nor to the farmed area. Despite the loss of marginal land, however, it seems inevitable to conclude that the increase in the area cultivated during the last decade has been associated with a decline in its average fertility.

POTENTIAL LAND

The question arises, 'How much more land could be brought under cultivation?'. Associated with this question is an ancillary one, 'What yields can be expected from such land?'. Several estimates have been made of the potential arable land in the world and they vary very considerably, from less than 2,000 million hectares which can be inferred from the Indicative World Plan of the FAO, to 3,687 million hectares in a report from the University of Wageningen, Holland. These extremes suggest that the world's arable acreage could be increased either by about 40% or to a value two and a half times the present one. Table 13 summarises some of the estimates. Revelle's (1976) estimate relies heavily on an investigation made by the US President's Science Advisory Committee and Revelle further states that with multiple cropping under irrigation the effective potential arable area is not 3,155 million hectares but 4,230 million. If Revelle's estimate of the total potential arable land in the world is correct – and there is no infallible means of knowing – then a comparison of Table 13 with Table 12 shows that this new land must come from present forest and pasture land. If the Wageningen estimate is correct, and if the pattern of land exploitation remains the same, then to realise the potential area of cultivated land will entail destruction of 50% of the world's forested areas and a further erosion of grazing lands. Nor is there any assurance that the breaking of new land will result in immediate success. Considerable problems have ensued in creating new cropped land on the so-called virgin soils of the Soviet Union, and attempts to grow grain on grasslands in Inner Mongolia have been a virtual failure.

There is little doubt that any new land that can be brought into

Table 13 *Estimates of potential agricultural land in the world*

Region	1980 cropped area	Potential cropped area (million ha) estimated wt			% of potentially cropped land at present cultivated		
		Club of Rome	Wageningen	Revelle	Club of Rome	Wageningen	Revelle
Developing countries	778	1,338	2,220	1,965	58	35	39
Developed countries	670	1,087	1,463	1,188	62	46	56
World	1,448	2,425	3,683	3,153	60	39	46

Sources: Club of Rome (Meadows *et al.*, 1972); Wageningen (Buringh *et al.*, 1975; De Hoog, 1976); Revelle, 1976.

cultivation will be poorer than the existing land in terms of its fertility. The major source of new land is from the reddish lateritic soils of the savannahs and forests of tropical and sub-tropical regions, the so-called latosols. These are low in basic mineral elements; many of the soils in the group are acid and they are usually deficient in phosphates (Webster and Wilson, 1980). For the reasons given earlier, the superior soils of the world have already come under cultivation. There is no counterpart of the North American continent to be brought into cultivation as there was in the nineteenth century. Yields on new land will on average be less than from those already cultivated.

WATER AND IRRIGATION

Semi-arid tropical and sub-tropical agricultures are susceptible to periodic droughts when rainfall is significantly less than the long-term average. With rain-fed farming in these areas, the sensitivity to this variation in rainfall is reflected in the variation in crop yield. The year-to-year variation in the yield of wheat may be taken as an example. Variation can be expressed as a coefficient of variation, that is the standard deviation of yield expressed as a percentage of the mean. In Europe the variability is about 10%. It is higher in Canada at about 15% for the Canadian wheat-growing areas are dependent on winter snowfall in the main for their moisture supply. In Australia variability rises to 18% while in Algeria and Morocco it approaches 25%. This means that the supply of wheat in the latter two countries can vary considerably from year to year. Even in the United States rare events can occur, associated with high temperatures and lack of rain, which wipe out crops entirely. An example was the experience in the western and southern parts of the corn-growing region in 1980. Extreme heat occurred at the time of flowering and pollination. Heat and drought caused premature flowering and fertilisation did not occur with the result that no grain was formed (McQuigg, 1981). Yield stability and the possibility of multiple cropping can be achieved in areas which are at the limit of viability of rain-fed agricultures by irrigation. Indeed, irrigation can convert the least promising of land and climatic resources into reasonably productive systems as the Israelis have demonstrated in the Negev where annual rainfall averages 50 mm, and is variable from year to year.

Irrigation involves watershed management, construction of dams (either large and coupled with power generation or quite small) and control of water (Peirera, 1974). Many schemes to harness river systems have been completed or are in progress in areas where rain is not sufficient to meet crop needs. Some are of considerable magnitude, an example being the Asswan High Dam to control the waters of the Nile. This scheme has been criticised; it has been stated that the incidence of bilharzia (schistosomiasis) along the Nile has increased, from 5% in 1937 to 35% and that, because of the retention of mud brought down by the Nile, Lake Nasser above the dam is silting up, the areas formerly flooded by the lower Nile are deprived of fertility and massive amounts of fertiliser have in consequence to be imported (Van der Schalie, 1974). More recent reports, however, state that the benefits from extended irrigation are considerable and the criticisms not well founded (Balba, 1983). There is certainly no doubt that irrigation presents considerable problems because of its proneness to mismanagement. Millions of hectares of land suffer from salination and Egypt is not immune from these problems since the irrigation water is free and over-irrigation is rife.

While water for irrigation is of considerable importance in any programmes to increase food production, water supplies are essential to man in a more direct way. The World Health Organisation has estimated that 50% of the world's population does not have access to a safe water supply. Safe in this sense means that the supply does not constitute a hazard to health. These hazards include not only diseases which are transmitted by consumption of contaminated water, such as the enteric diseases, but also diseases which are transmitted by contact with water such as bilharzia, and the diseases which are insect borne and are transmitted to man by insects breeding in or near water. Examples in the latter category are African trypanosomiasis, onchocerciasis and malaria. The provision of safe water is as essential to progress as is the provision of adequate and better diets.

There are considerable problems with respect to the large-scale use of natural river drainage systems. These are in part political. Fifty of the world's rivers or fresh water lakes are shared by more than four countries and almost 150 rivers and lakes are shared by two or more countries. Obviously the construction of a dam upstream to one country can cause considerable difficulties in a second country downstream.

FOOD SYSTEMS

Provision of water for drinking and for sanitation, and of fuel for cooking cannot really be separated from provision of the food itself in any consideration of present or likely future resources. The concept of a food system embraces the various component parts of the overall process of providing nourishment. The variation in the complexity of food provision systems throughout the world is immense. At the one extreme is the self-contained peasant family at subsistence level, obtaining its food from its own labour, its water from a local source, its fuel from forays into adjacent wooded areas and only dependent on local markets for essential items such as salt and cooking oil. At the other extreme are food systems such as our own in which there are producers of commodities, manufacturers of food, wholesale and retail distributors of food, centralised provision of water, sewage and garbage disposal, and in which fuel for cooking is provided by centrally generated electricity or distributed gas. The whole of the latter extreme system involves considerable investment of capital and massive transport capability. In between these extremes is a variety of systems, and generally, as urbanisation proceeds, the complexity of food systems augments.

ENERGY ACCOUNTING OF FOOD SYSTEMS

A convenient way in which these systems can be examined is through energy accounting, that is by estimating the expenditure of primary fuels necessary to make the systems work. The conventions employed are simple. The energy ascribed to the primary fuels are their heats of combustion less the energy expended to acquire them. The energy value of coal is thus its heat of combustion less the energy expended in mining it and bringing it to the surface, while the energy cost of electricity generated from coal is the energy cost of the coal at pit head less the energy cost of transport of coal to the power station, the losses which take place in converting coal to power and the losses that occur in transmission lines.

Table 14 gives, as an example, the approach applied to the United Kingdom food system (Blaxter, 1977). The agricultural sector which is concerned with the production of commodities accounts for about a fifth of the total support energy cost of the system and the industrial processing, importation, wholesaling

Table 14 *Support energy used in the United Kingdom food system*

	J × 10^{15}/annum		% of total
Agriculture	360	420	18
Animal feed import	60		
Food industry	527	1,186	50
Food import	208		
Food distribution	451		
House expenditure	728	754	32
Garbage and sewage	26		
Total	2,360		100
Food requirement of the population	241		
Ratio primary fuel expenditure/human food consumed	= 9.8		

and retailing of food accounts for half. The total amount of energy expended in the system is enormous and can be put into perspective by relating it to the energy which the population obtains from food. This is 240 × 10^{15} J and for every MJ of energy we consume as food we expend almost 10 MJ of support energy, most of which comes from oil, coal, natural gas and uranium, for we have relatively little hydro-electrical generating capacity. Other highly developed societies have a similar profligate expenditure of support energy to sustain their food provision system. In the United States the support energy required to provide 1 MJ of food on the plate is larger than that in the United Kingdom; in Israel and in Australia it is slightly less. The support energy expended in the food provision system is about 28% of the total support energy used in the United Kingdom. By contrast, and at the other extreme, the support energy required by self-contained peasant societies is negligibly small. Obviously there is a gradation between the two extremes of the support energy dependence of food provision systems, and equally obvious, as urbanisation grows so the support energy dependence of the food systems of peoples will tend to increase, if only because food has to be transported, processed in bulk and stored before sale, and because an infrastructure of food-related services has to be provided.

SUPPORT ENERGY AND AGRICULTURE

The agricultural component of the food provision system is of most concern. As already mentioned, the dependence of modern agricultures on support energy is a relatively recent phenomenon. It has been associated with considerable increases in the yields of crops and has been called the second agricultural revolution since, after stagnation of yields for almost a century, suddenly, in the late 1930s and 1940s yields commenced to rise, to more than double in a quarter of a century. One of the most detailed studies of the time course of this change is that undertaken in Norway (NLVF, 1984). In the period from 1929 to 1979 the use of support energy in Norway's agriculture increased by a factor of 4.5. Table 15 summarises the changes which took place in 50 years expressed as the amounts of land, labour and support energy necessary to produce 1 MJ of human food. Less land was needed in 1979 compared with 1929 and less labour too, but this was at the expense of a threefold increase in the expenditure of support energy. Yields per hectare have increased and so has productivity per man, but every MJ of food energy produced now takes 4 MJ of support energy expended on the farm alone, a figure higher than the similar one for the United Kingdom that may be calculated from the values in Table 14.

The support energy used in agriculture consists of fuel for tractors and other farm machinery, the energy used in extracting mineral fertiliser from deposits or manufacturing nitrogenous fertiliser from the nitrogen of the air – an energy-demanding process – the energy cost of making other agrochemicals, of providing transport of essential goods to the farm and the energy costs of manufacturing the tractors, ploughs, combine harvesters

Table 15 *The use of labour, land and support energy in food production from agriculture in Norway (values expressed per unit of food energy produced with 1929 = 100)*

	1929	1949	1979
Commercial energy/MJ food	100	153	309
Land/MJ food	100	83	63
Labour/MJ food	100	80	25

and other machinery and implements required. The proportional make up of the total varies from one country and one type of farming to another depending on the cropping and stocking policies, but in the most advanced agricultures, fertilisers and chemicals usually make up a quarter to a third of the total, direct fuel costs varying somewhat reciprocally. Energy accounting can be taken to the level of individual commodities (see Pimmental and Pimmental, 1979) when it is found that to produce one unit of energy edible by man from animal enterprises requires ten times as much support energy as does production of one unit from a cropping enterprise. Furthermore, as the intensity of livestock farming increases, and as livestock become more and more separated from land, as exemplified by intensive methods of pig and poultry production, the greater becomes this difference in support energy requirement.

AGRICULTURE'S SHARE OF SUPPORT ENERGY

In Norway's case, agriculture accounted for 4% of the country's total support energy consumption in 1929 and 4.9% in 1979. In the instance of the United Kingdom, agriculture currently accounts for 3.6% of the total. The FAO has made a wide study of support energy in the agricultural sectors of most countries of the world and the results of their analysis are given in Table 16. They

Table 16 *Support energy in agriculture in different regions of the world (FAO)*

Region	Total energy	Energy in agriculture	% in agriculture	Total energy per capita	Agricultural energy per agricultural worker
	$J \times 10^{18}$			$J \times 10^{9}$	
Developed market economies	135.7	4.6	3.4	184	108
North America	76.9	2.1	2.8	333	559
Western Europe	42.9	2.1	4.9	119	82
Oceania	2.4	0.1	5.6	154	247
East Europe with USSR	49.8	1.6	3.3	141	29
Total – developed countries	185.5	6.3	3.4	170	62
Developing market economies	19.3	0.9	4.8	11	2
Africa	1.6	0.1	4.5	5	1
Latin America	8.1	0.3	3.8	28	9
Far East	7.0	0.4	5.3	6	1
Near East	2.6	0.2	6.4	24	4
Asian centrally planned economies	14.3	0.4	2.9	17	2
Total – developing countries	33.6	1.3	4.0	13	2
Total – world	219.1	7.6	3.5	59	10

show that in the world as a whole the use of support energy in agriculture averages 3.6% of the total. More striking is the fact that there is little variation between countries in the proportion of their national energy consumption that is used in agriculture. The proportion is the same in the poorer countries as in the richer ones.

This situation raises some important issues, as can be inferred from the following general statements. There is a close positive relationship between the wealth of a country as measured by its gross domestic product and its consumption of support energy. There is little doubt that the massive increase in productivity of land that has come about in the developed countries of the world has been due to the use of support energy. A fairly constant proportion of every country's energy supplies are devoted to the food-producing sector. These statements show that there is a link between overall economic development and agricultural development, and that enhanced food production can only come about as the economies of countries improve overall, when more support energy is consumed per capita and when more is devoted to agriculture.

It is axiomatic that the fossil fuel reserves of the world are finite. They represent past aeons of photosynthesis and one can estimate that known reserves are equivalent only to the amount of solar radiation that impinges on the outer atmosphere of the earth in two years. One of the fossil fuels, and plainly the most convenient, oil, is already causing concern in the world because its procurement is becoming more and more expensive. The alternative energy supply from nuclear installations is fraught with many difficulties which, we can now appreciate, were initially underestimated, while there is a limit to the generation of electricity from river systems. The assumption that the developing countries can industrialise and in doing so develop economies which are as demanding on energy resources as our own is dubious. Equally it is hardly reasonable to suggest that those countries should develop support energy dependent food systems when we ourselves are – or should be – worried about their long-term viability.

SOME CONCLUSIONS

Despite the many uncertainties we can state that in the immediate future agricultural production should be increased considerably and an increase of 75% before the turn of the century seems a reasonable estimate of what should be the aim. Beyond the end of the century forecasting becomes a highly tenuous activity.

The two means available for increasing production which we have, namely bringing more land into cultivation and increasing production from unit area, both entail difficulties. The one can destroy other resources immediately essential to man, namely the forest areas, and the other seemingly commits the world to an exploitative technology, largely based on use of the fossil fuel reserves of the world. One can argue that the pessimism of Malthus was largely dispelled in the nineteenth and early twentieth century by increasing the land resource consequent upon the opening up of new lands in the Americas, Australasia and Southern Africa. In the last half century the pessimism has been further attenuated by the success achieved in increasing yield per unit area through the use of energy derived from past eras of photosynthesis to augment that currently produced. There is at present no sign of some new and additional delaying tactic that could be employed to postpone Malthus' vista.

6

People in the developing countries

POPULATIONS AND PEOPLE

The previous chapters have dealt with the population of the developing world as a whole, sometimes distinguishing geographical regions, and only occasionally mentioning individual countries and then merely to illustrate a particular point on a reasonable scale. Every country of the ninety or so which comprise the whole has its singular problems and difficulties. The collective terms, 'the third world', 'the south', or 'the less well developed countries' include a wide variety of human situations. Even within a country there can be massive divisions. In Nigeria, for example, the main ethnic one is between the Moslem Hausa and Fulani in the north of the country and the predominantly Christian Ibo and Yoruba in the south. These are two groupings which have contrasting cultures, attitudes, and economic status. In addition there are smaller groups – the Tiv and the Kanuri – as well as immigrants from the Ashanti peoples. The internal diversity of ethnic groups, cultures, languages and religions contributes to a structural instability in Nigeria illustrated by the Biafran war and more recently by the campaign to expel immigrants from Ghana. The same sorts of divisions are evident in the populations of Zimbabwe where political parties have coalesced largely on former tribal lines, and it is little to be wondered that serious and disruptive wars, civil disturbances or coups have taken place in at least twenty African countries in the last two decades. They are still taking place in those areas of the Sahel where problems of food supply are the most acute. It has, however, to be remembered that many of the tribal groupings in

Africa formerly had traditions of war, notable examples being the Zulu of Natal and the armoured horsemen of Bornu in West Africa. Such traditions die hard. The rise of fanatical Moslem movements such as the Dervish brotherhood of the Sanusi and later that associated with the Mahdi in the Sudan, were also associated with wars which transcended tribal boundaries.

Some of the blame for the internal conflicts must be taken by the former colonial powers. The concept of colonial dependencies and empire paid scant heed to tribal distribution. As Damman (1979) has remarked: 'In 1884 at the last Colonization Conference in Berlin, the big powers divided Africa among themselves, and drew arbitrary lines across the lands of black people without consideration of language or ethnic groups.' These dividing lines have hardly been altered in the last century. At least on the partition of British India an attempt was made to separate the main groups – the Hindu and the Moslem – but as recent events have shown other groupings, notably the Sikhs, were ignored. The persistence of loyalties of people to former structures, and the strength of religious ties cannot be minimised; one has only to think of the identities of people in the British Isles, or in the United Kingdom to realise that this is not simply a phenomenon of the developing countries of the world. Certainly, as the colonial powers have withdrawn, so a new sense of nationalism (or a resuscitation of an older one) has emerged, leading to an inexorable growth in the number of member states in the United Nations' family.

LAND OWNERSHIP AND THE LANDLESS PEOPLE

It is because of the complexity of the structure of countries within the developing world and the large variation between them that generalisations are somewhat meaningless and often naive. Even so some can be made. An obvious one is that the structures of their societies, formerly very stable, are undergoing considerable change. Tribal and extended-family loyalties are being replaced by social structures which are more akin to those in capitalist countries of the western world, the countries which are usually referred to as the developed market economies. Economic development and technological change in food production methods have in many instances been synchronous with an acceptance of western social mores. Perhaps the best example relates to land ownership and tenure. In sub-Saharan Africa, land was in the past owned by the tribe and allocated to individuals within it. A transition has taken place from tribal to individual right of ownership with the inevitable consequence of accumulation of land by a few, imposition of punitive rents, evictions and absentee landlordism. Farms have increased in size. In Kenya farms larger than 100 hectares now account for a fifth of the total agricultural production, while more than half the country's farmers occupy holdings which are less than 2 hectares in extent, and this land accounts for only 15% of the total cropped land. Farm size is also increasing in Bangladesh where 11% of the population now owns over half the land. Freehold occupation of land may encourage progressive farming, but much evidence suggests that economies of scale do not necessarily occur and output per unit land does not necessarily increase. In Bangladesh, surveys of households show that food energy and food protein consumption are negatively correlated with land concentration and evidence from Thailand shows that rice yield per hectare is greater on farms of 1–2 hectares than it is on larger ones of 50 hectares or more (University of Dhaka, 1981).

The World Food Council of the United Nations, which was established following the World Food Conference of 1974, expressed concern at its meeting in June 1983 about the emergence of a dualistic structure of food production in the developing world, in which a large and traditional subsistence farming sector was bypassed by large-scale farming. It commented: 'As a result the absolute numbers of undernourished people have increased and their proportion may have increased as well.' Concentration of land concentrates income into fewer hands; it does not necessarily distribute wealth and well-being.

URBANISATION

The effect of this concentration of land into fewer hands, coupled with population growth and land shortage has been to erode former extended-family structures and to create a class of landless people, who are the poorest of the poor. In Africa and in Asia the idea of family is much wider than that in the United Kingdom. It includes quite distant relatives and kin, indeed it is more analogous to a clan than a family. The ethic involves an obligation of the individual to the group, and in the absence of any national scheme for support provides a social insurance. With reduction in the amount of land per capita this system breaks down. The FAO of the United Nations has estimated that in non-communist Asia some 30% of rural people are now without land, some of them being employed on larger farms, some existing through the family links. Many of the landless, however, migrate to urban areas where the abject poverty of the shanty towns bears witness to the fact that they are not only landless but jobless too. Many of these people are semi-literate at best and they certainly have no skills which could lead to industrial employment. And, with their ties to their rural background cut, the family net of social security has been foregone.

In instances some of these landless people attempt to create new land to farm. In the semi-arid zones this involves attempts to farm on inadequate resources of soil and moisture, with predictable consequences. The viability of such enterprises in years in which rainfall is only marginally below the long-term average is negligible. The more usual step is internal migration to the towns and cities. Urbanisation is occurring in virtually all countries of the world as shown by the higher annual increments of urban than of total population. In Mexico, for example, the rate of urban growth from 1970 to 1982 was 4.2%, considerably greater than the growth rate of the population as a whole which was 3%. In India the comparable figures were 3.9% for urban growth and 2.3% for total population growth. The strain that this growth places on the infrastructures of cities in the developing world is obvious; it is equally obvious that the growth of the urban population reduces the land available for food production.

These landless people are impoverished in countries which are poor. The mean gross national product per capita in Bangladesh is $140 per year, a figure which may be contrasted with our own of $9,700 and that of the United States of $13,200. This mean income includes those of many who have an income of less than $12 per year, and this group includes those who receive no income at all and scavenge for food. Surveys show that none of the children of parents in this income group go to school. Income has to be more than $150 per year before 50% of the children receive any education. At the other end of the scale there are many in Bangladesh who have standards of living similar to our own.

PEASANT FARMERS

It is those in what the World Food Council terms 'the traditional subsistence sector' of the population who should concern us most. They and the landless are either trapped by the changes in the social structure or are vulnerable to change. The view taken by many economists is that change is both desirable and necessary for survival. Bauer and Yamey (1972) have written, 'The family system acts as a serious obstacle to economic progress. A man is much less likely to be willing and able to rise in the income scale and to save and invest, when he knows that, should he succeed in improving his position, he would have to maintain a large number of distant relatives, distant in the sense of having remote blood ties and quite often in the sense that they live far away.' There is, however, a resistance to these desirable and necessary changes regarded as essential to economic progress. Peasant societies do not necessarily respond to economic pressures in the ways people respond in developed societies. Possibilities of increased income do not necessarily lead to greater effort or demand since habits of consumption are ingrained and there is, in any event, a limited range of goods available to meet an augmented demand or to encourage it. Working less is a response to higher return in many of these societies, for leisure is valued. Attitudes to children and the family group reflect this and the somewhat egocentric attributes extolled by Bauer and Yamey are not much in evidence. Children provide not only an insurance against old age but from early childhood provide supplementary labour for the less physically demanding tasks in food production. This latter assessment of peasant attitudes was first articulated by the Russian economist, A. V. Chayanov in a seminal book *The Theory of Non-Capitalistic Economic Systems*. An account of this work is given by Grigg (1980).

All the evidence, however, shows that peasants will behave like the conventional economic man given sufficient pressure. They will adopt new agricultural technologies, use new varieties of crop plant, and augment fertiliser use to increase their productivity and income. In so doing they are, however, changing their whole attitude to life and adopting goals that are in the main alien to their older, traditional culture. If they aspire to western norms, then the distance that they perceive between themselves and the sophisticated elite in their own countries must seem to them immense and virtually insuperable.

ACCOMMODATION TO CHANGE

In adapting to western modes of food production it appears that peasant societies have accepted some features and rejected others. In much of the developing world peasant farmers depend wholly on hand labour. Table 17 shows for large regions of the developing world the present dependence on machine, animal and manpower for the work done in the fields. In the United Kingdom virtually all field work is undertaken by tractors; the horse is no longer an agricultural animal and direct manpower is limited to a very small horticultural component. The advantage of mechanising agriculture is that field operations are speeded up. A 50 horse-power tractor can till a hectare in about 5 hours. A pair of oxen take about 60 hours and if the same task is undertaken by hand 400 hours of heavy work are involved. Speed is important since it transfers to a timeliness of farm operation, a matter often of crucial importance in multiple cropping ventures with their large seasonal peaks of demand for power. Speed is equally important in some types of rain-fed agricultures where there is but a short 'window' of weather during which field operations are possible. The difficulties for most developing countries is the high cost in terms of fuel. In any event, replacing hand labour by machine power, while it increases food output per man, exacerbates the problems of rural unemployment. In some instances there may be little or no increase in output per unit area of land. An example is the displacement of the hand labour formerly used to weed vegetable crops in Hong Kong. Herbicides and flame throwers were employed; labour was saved but there was no change in yield per hectare.

It is now generally accepted that in the initial stages of development of peasant agricultures it is undesirable to stress the importance of transfer of the technology of agricultural mechanisation. It does seem sensible, however, and indeed humane to relieve some of the sheer drudgery of field work through provision of mechanical aid. Small tractors have not, however, proved successful in many developing countries, an exception being the People's Republic of China. Generally, costs outweigh advantages and the capital cost of a 5 h.p. tractor is beyond the means of most.

Modernisation of agriculture involves, in addition to mechanisation, the use of artificial fertilisers to augment yield, and, at a later stage, adoption of new varieties of crop plant which can respond to the higher levels of soil fertility brought about by fertiliser application. In the world as a whole the current use of fertiliser is 80 kg per hectare and half the fertiliser applied is nitrogenous. In the developed countries the average rate of application is 123 kg per hectare and in the developing ones 33 kg. What is remarkable is that in the Asian centrally planned

Table 17 *The use of manpower, animal power and tractor power by farmers in regions of the developing world (percentage of the reliance placed on the power source)*

	Region			
Source of power	Africa	Far East	Near East	Latin America
Man	86	72	65	62
Animal	9	23	15	13
Tractor	3	3	20	25

economies fertiliser use is at a greater rate – 146 kg per hectare – than it is in the developed world. In China, where 80% of the fertiliser applied is nitrogenous, the support energy represented by the total fertiliser input now exceeds that similarly employed in Europe.

It thus appears that, very sensibly, most developing countries have selected the one component of the compendium of agricultural technologies dependent on support energy which does not reduce labour inputs but increases yield per unit land. These policies are continuing. Tanzania, for example, is devoting one entire field of her new-found reserve of natural gas to the fuelling of an ammonia plant (UNDP, 1983). The infrastructure of credit facilities, transport and technical knowledge of crop requirements in specific locations has to be improved if further advances on these lines are to be made. In some developing countries foreign exchange for construction of plant and provision of facilities are limiting, but most realise that increased use of fertilisers is a necessary step to increasing productivity.

That fertilisers are being employed on this scale certainly shows that the peasant farmer responds to the availability of new inputs to increase his output. This might suggest that he is responding in the responsible way expected of people in a market economy. Motivation cannot be assumed. The uneducated are not stupid and the adoption of this facet of modern agricultural technology may simply reflect a desire to provide for his expanded family at previous levels rather than a commitment to the profit motive in its conventional sense.

Progress as we understand it is inhibited by grinding poverty, the adherence to values conditioned by past experience and the lack of education within a society which has been eroded and is subject to religious and other constraints. Our understanding of progress involves the division of labour, industrialisation to provide desirable goods, urbanisation of the major part of the work force, a consumer society and a western European culture. Progress in this sense might appear to have been made in Taiwan and in South Korea, but in those countries progress may simply be an expression of a new colonialism and may not be deeply rooted.

SOME CONCLUSIONS

There is no doubt that in the last fifty years or more the developed world has contributed much to the peoples of the developing one. The major contribution has been in terms of the prolongation of the life of the individual, and nothing can minimise this. To have eradicated smallpox from the whole globe is a magnificent contribution to the well-being of man. Control of disease by protective innoculation or by simple medical procedures was readily carried out. Now, the problems are more complex and more difficult. The control of water-borne disease and the provision of sufficient food for an enlarged population entails transfers of technologies which are far from easy and transfers which acknowledge that each and every small community needs a separate analysis and consideration. In particular, the constraints on developing food production and in combating hunger are as much social as technical ones.

7

Limits and resources

THE LIMITS TO THE YIELDS OF CROPS

When the algebraic expression of Malthus' contentions was explored in Chapter 2, the concept of the carrying capacity of an area of land was introduced. This concept can be enlarged to include the world as a whole and the question asked, 'How many people could the land resources of the world really support?' Neglecting for the moment the needs of man for biological products other than food, the answer obviously depends on the area of land which can be made to yield food and the yield per unit area. The potential land area of the world has already been discussed; here consideration is given to the potential yield of crops per hectare of land.

Two estimates of potential yield can be employed. The first is simply the maximal yields ever recorded for particular crops, that is yields which represent what can be achieved through superlative husbandry, using optimal inputs of fertilisers and agrochemicals. Some of these record yields for different crops are summarised in Table 18 from which it is clear that they depart from average yields very considerably. It can also be inferred that there is considerable potential for increasing the average yield of these crops on a world-wide basis. The second approach is to calculate the yield which can be expected from the solar radiation intercepted, using modern knowledge about the biological factors involved in the transduction of the energy of solar radiation to that of the organic molecules which the plant synthesises. It is assumed that there are no limitations placed upon the plants by shortages of nutrients or water and that they

Table 18 *World record yields of crops and yields in the developed and developing countries of the world in 1983**

Crop	World record yield t/ha	Mean yield in 1983 Developed countries	Mean yield in 1983 Developing countries	Highest yield for a country in 1983	
Wheat	14	2.30	1.98	Netherlands	7.04
Rice	14	5.26	3.05	Korea P.R.	6.34
Maize	20	4.41	1.95	Greece	9.59
Sorghum	22	2.64	1.17	Israel	4.60
Potatoes	100	15.44	11.94	Israel	43.77
Cassava	77	—	8.28	India	15.87
Sweet potatoes	41	16.00	14.50	Korea P.R.	24.00
Yam	45	13.70	4.30	Japan	17.53
Soya beans	4.5	1.69	1.50	Italy	3.20
Ground nuts	10	2.05	1.00	Malaysia	3.51

*Excluding countries growing less than 5000 ha of the crop.

are free of competition from weeds and immune to attack from fungal or viral disease or from pests. The calculation is thus one which represents the ultimate theoretical potential of the plant in producing food.

The wheat crop in the United Kingdom can be taken to illustrate this second approach and the results of the calculations are given in Table 19. The results are perhaps surprising. Maximally, only 0.75% of the solar radiation received is harvested as grain. This quantity corresponds to a yield of wheat of 15.6 tonnes per hectare. It is equally surprising that the record wheat yield which was obtained by Mr Rennie in Midlothian is 90% of this ultimate limit to yield. The average yield of wheat in the United Kingdom is 6.2 tonnes per hectare which is about 40% of the ultimate limit. As a generalisation it can be stated that most of the record yields obtained for other crops are also close to 90% of the ultimate theoretical yield calculated for the latitudes in which they can be grown. Yields for maize grain and for sorghum in

Table 19 *The theoretical maximal production of wheat per hectare of land in the United Kingdom**

Component	Factor %	Cumulative %
Annual incoming solar radiation	—	100
Correction for length of year crop occupies the land	0.66	66
Correction for the photosynthetically active component of radiation	0.48	32
Efficiency of photosynthesis	0.20	6.3
Correction for photo-respiration	0.70	4.4
Correction for kinetics of light saturation	0.70	3.1
Correction for 'dark' respiration for biosynthesis of complex molecules and for maintenance	0.60	1.9
Correction for weight of roots	0.90	1.7
Correction for ratio grain/shoot	0.45	0.75†

*This calculation assumes that there are no constraints due to lack of water or sail nutrients or the presence of pests and diseases. The incoming solar radiation is taken to be 33×10^{12} J.
†Equivalent to 13.4 t/ha dry weight of grain or 15.6 t/ha of wheat with the conventional 14% moisture.

Table 18 reflect not only that they are crops of lower latitudes than wheat, but also that they have a slightly different mode of photosynthesis, while the higher yields of dry matter which can be inferred to have been obtained from root crops reflects the fact that translocation of the photosynthate into roots or swollen stems is a more efficient process than storage in seeds.

ARE THE LIMITS ABSOLUTE?

The two estimates of potential, one from records of accomplishments and the other from theoretical calculations, can be regarded as estimates of limits to the biological productivity of land, the first based on records being perhaps the more acceptable. Such limits are of course calculated for existing crop plants.

The possibility that the potential of existing plants could be increased is present, but the probability that genetic improvement could lead to a massive raising of the limits to crop yield appears remote. With the cereals, including the rices of the green revolution, the spectacular increases in yield which have taken place in the last two decades has largely come about through the exploitation of dwarfing genes. Dwarf cereals translocate more of the photosynthate to the grain and less to the straw, and because of their habit of growth they are able to utilise larger amounts of fertiliser without falling flat. The dwarfing genes concerned have, however, for the most part been exploited. The remaining possibilities of increasing the limits to yield reside in alterations to the efficiency of the photosynthetic process itself, an incredibly difficult task of genetic engineering – if indeed such a task can be accomplished at all. This does not of course mean that there will not be signal advances in the breeding of crop plants. New genetic advances will be made to produce cultivars which have resistance to cold, soil salinity, drought, pests and diseases. Their use will enable marginal land to be farmed and will increase total production as a result, but they will not increase the limits set by the thermodynamic processes of the green leaf in converting solar energy to human food.

There are other ways, however, in which yield could be increased. One is to increase the carbon dioxide content of the atmosphere surrounding the crop plant. There is much experience of undertaking this with crops under glass when yield can be enhanced very considerably. Whether such steps can be taken with field crops is doubtful; it has, however, to be remembered that a considerable part – probably a quarter – of the increase in crop yield which has taken place in the last fifty years can be attributed to the increase in the partial pressure of carbon dioxide in the atmosphere which has arisen from the burning of fossil fuels. Another possibility of extending limits is to consider new types of plant altogether, particularly plants which do not shed their leaves annually. The efficiency of coniferous forests in using solar radiation is much higher than that of crop plants, largely because their canopies are completely closed, implying that almost all incoming radiation is intercepted throughout the year, and because the life duration of their leaves is long. Whether new perennial crop plants with a high yield of potential human food could be developed is necessarily conjectural. Limits might also be raised by removal of the constraints placed on crop growth by high or low temperatures. Their effects could be combated by engineering developments on a massive scale. The cost in terms of expenditure of wealth would be considerable but would increase output from land which is limited by these climatic hazards. Such a step could conceivably increase the ultimate limit of yield. Generally it would seem that the possibilities of increasing the ultimate ceiling on crop yield are somewhat remote. It follows that the carrying capacity of land is not likely to be enhanced very much through large improvements in the intrinsic efficiency of crop plants.

THE CARRYING CAPACITY OF THE EARTH

There have been many estimates made of the number of people that could be supported by the earth, commencing with that by Ravenstein in 1891 (see Gilland, 1983). Some of them have been summarised in Table 20. What is remarkable about this table is the considerable range of the estimates. Some authorities suggest that the world could support but 50% more people while others imply that over thirty times as many as at present could be accommodated. This gross variation can largely be explained by the differences in the assumptions made. Thus de Wit took a high estimate of potential land and an estimate of biological productivity based on theoretical calculations of the amount of carbohydrate synthesised from the incoming solar radiation in each latitude, that is an estimate of yield which was the ultimate attainable. This, from later work at Wageningen appears to be equivalent to a yield of grain or its equivalent of 14.6 tonnes per hectare. Revelle used a lower estimate of 5 tonnes per hectare on a larger potential arable area to arrive at a lower figure while

Table 20 *Some estimates of the maximal number of people the world could support*

Authority	Millions	Ratio of maximal number to present number
De facto population (1980)	4,414	
Ravenstein (1871)	6,000	1.4
Penck (1925)	16,000	3.6
Brown, Bonner and Weir (1957)	7,000	1.6
Clark (1967) low estimate	47,000	10.7
Clark (1967) high estimate	150,000	33.9
De Wit (1967)	146,000	33.0
Buringh and Van Heemst (1972)	6,700	1.5
Lieth (1972)	100,000	22.7
Revelle (1976)	40,000	9.1
Eyre (1978)	17,000	4.1
Gilland (1983)	7,500	1.7

Gilland used Revelle's yield limits for different climatic regions and combined them with a lowered estimate of potential cropped land. Some of the lower estimates recognise that man does not live by food alone. Thus Eyre computed that human needs comprised 1,000 kg of organic matter as food and a further 500 kg for paper, timber and forest products. Others have considered food alone. The lower of Clark's two estimates makes provision for diets including a high proportion of animal products; most other estimates appear based on the contention that the diet is based entirely on food from plants. Some of the estimates included allowances for urban and recreational use on potential arable land; in others no such provision is made.

The differences in assumptions appear to explain the very large differences between the estimates. To arrive at any measure of carrying capacity thus involves a choice of assumptions. Some of those associated with the more extreme estimates can be examined. Commencing with the highest estimates, it does not seem reasonable to suppose that all land can produce crops at the rates which are commensurate with the solar radiation input and the theoretical ultimate efficiency of its capture. Nor does it seem likely that all farms can achieve yields which are equal to those of farmers who at present hold records. Such farms that have produced record yields have soils of higher intrinsic fertility, and while limitations due to fertility differences could be overcome by technical measures, it is unlikely that all would have the considerable managerial and technical skill to do so. Furthermore, in any one growing season it is usual to find that the variation of yield from farm to farm in an area is about 20% for cereal crops. It seems unlikely that this sort of variation could occur around a crop mean equal to that of record holders. It thus seems that the highest of the estimates of the carrying capacity of the world can be dismissed as theoretically interesting but practically highly unlikely. At the other extreme the lower limit to average yield must be more than the present one. There are vast areas where by adoption of more intensive methods of farming – which implies a greater use of resources external to the farm – yield could be signally increased. What the potential yield of crops on some future cropped area is likely to be is thus a matter for conjecture. The highest and lowest estimates can be dismissed as either improbable or too pessimistic. All that can be concluded is that the carrying capacity of the world cannot be expressed with any certainty.

Even so, what is certain is that there are limits. Limits are set by the land area which determines the earth's interception of photosynthetically active radiation, by the efficiency of photosynthesis and by the support energy required to ensure that the biological systems on which we depend work at high efficiency. This conclusion leads to another. There must be a limit to the human population when numbers reach the carrying capacity of the land. This general statement is in complete accord with Malthus' view. There can be no equivocation about it. Where there is uncertainty it is about the precise definition of the limit to the number of people that can be supported, about the way in which population will augment, about the rate at which food production will approach the limit set by carrying capacity and about the availability of resources to fuel the latter approach.

SOME ECONOMIC POINTS OF VIEW

In this and previous chapters food, land and population have been discussed largely in a conceptual framework which is biologically oriented. When considering how resources are employed, however, it is reasonable to consider the views of these wide problems taken by economists. Here difficulties abound. As Pearce (1976) has remarked, there are 'contrasts, incompatibilities and inconsistencies' in the approaches taken by economists and non-economists to such problems. Pearce has gone much further and referred to 'the arrogant attitude of scientists in commenting on economics, a subject about which many of them seem to possess astronomic ignorance' and to 'the essentially conservative and non-objective nature of ecology as a science or mode of thinking, ill suited to serve as the basis for developing the central public policies of the world'. He concluded 'that either mutual understanding of scientists and economists was at fault, or, if their approaches are truly incompatible, that it is essential to find out which is true, since this matters a great deal in resource allocation'. Clearly any discussion of economics by a biologist has to be undertaken with care and circumspection!

Within every discipline there are schools of thought, more perhaps in economics than in the biological sciences, and it is indeed probable that many scientists are as bewildered by economic theories as are economists by biological ones. Such are the problems that beset mankind that one must agree with Pearce that effort should be made to foster understanding, difficult though this may be, because modes of thought and methods of enquiry differ so much between scientists and economists. Before dealing with resource allocation and the difficult problems relating to the use of land, it is perhaps useful to summarise some of the economic theories about the broader aspects of the relation between the numbers of people and their food supply. Some of these have been dealt with earlier when the reactions to Malthus' essay were discussed in chapter 2. The more recent approaches equally merit examination.

Perhaps the least contentious of issues with which to commence is with the views of Ester Boserup (1965). These owe much to those of Chayonov on the nature of peasant societies which do not conform to the classical economic concept of 'economic man in the market place'. She contends that population increase is the spur to technological innovation in food production. Her argument is that in the initial stages of population growth, peasant societies increase the area which they cultivate but this process does not lead to an increase in labour productivity, that is in the output of food per head of the peasant's family or extended family. As population rises, food prices also rise to induce some farmers to intensify production and to innovate. The adoption of the potato as a food staple in Ireland was taken by Boserup as an example of this idea that population growth acts as a spur to technological development. It is her view that the growth of population transforms peasant societies into market economies. Throughout the process – except perhaps for local difficulty – population will be in an equilibrium with the food supply. Her model states nothing about whether this equilibrium, which is changing over time, ever attains stability.

Other studies have been made by economists of the problem of population equilibrium. One is of considerable interest for it purports to show that two equilibria can occur, one, the so called low-level equilibrium trap and the other a higher equilibrium that leads to economic growth. The first takes place when an increase in living standards encourages growth of numbers rather than a growth in individual income. The second, higher equilibrium point is attained if an increase in income results in a further increase in income the rate of which exceeds population growth (Moreland and Hazeldine, 1974). The basic premises on which this model is built are that population growth declines with increase in level of income and that the rate of increase of income increases with the level of income. The first premise accords with one explanation of the population changes which have taken place in the countries with developed market economies. The second seems to accord with the contention that to him that hath shall be given. To overcome the low-level trap, massive amounts of capital are required from external sources since capital cannot be generated within an economy in such a state. The conclusion appears reasonable enough, but the premises are somewhat dubious. As pointed out in Chapter 2, a description of what took place in the last demographic cycle in Europe does not enable one to predict what will occur in the future in a developing country. Additionally, there is evidence to suggest that income growth does not necessarily increase with level of income in some regions. The shape of the relationships between numbers of people and income and between rate of change of income and its level, are critical to the theory.

FOOD AND WEALTH

Economists are criticised not only by fellow economists but also by scientists. One criticism that biologically minded people make is that economists 'see the world as a commodity' (McHarg, 1969). This is perhaps best exemplified by the concept of wealth and particularly by Eyre's (1978) concept of wealth as described in *The Real Wealth of Nations*. Eyre computed the primary production of organic matter in the world from estimates of the productivity of natural ecosystems and under annual cropping. It was this aspect of his computation which was included in Table 20. Eyre, however, added to these estimates the food equivalent of a country's mineral wealth. This was computed from the relative prices of food and minerals. One can ask immediately what these prices are likely to be in the future, thus implying that his concept of wealth may have no long-term validity. One can ask how to eat bauxite, or question the value of a mixture of manganese ore and oranges in the year 2084. Such a concept of wealth has meaning only within a current context of demand and price for commodities. Zambia's copper resource illustrates this point. On independence in 1964, Zambia simply 'Zambianised' the exploitative structures for copper extraction which had been developed by commercial interests under the former colonial power. She aspired to a rapid acquisition of western norms of life and she neglected her agriculture. Her development and her food provision system were bound to the world price of copper. As the world price of copper fell relative to those of other goods, services and food, so she became heavily in debt. Initially Zambia was rich; now she is poor.

RESOURCE ECONOMICS

Zambia must have made decisions about how to allocate resources as between industry and agriculture when she achieved independence. So too did India when she decided to give greater emphasis to industry than to agriculture (Mellor, 1976). Mao Tse Tung made it perfectly clear that in the early years of the People's Republic of China, priority was to be given to agriculture and to light industry located in the countryside. Allocations of resources is a branch of economics – resource economics – which is now well explored after having been neglected for a century or more. Resources can be broadly classified into those which are renewable and those which are not, finer distinctions being added which relate to the extent to which resources are recycled and the services they require to maintain them. In one area, fisheries management, there has been a happy synthesis of the ideas of biologists dealing with the growth and population dynamics of fish and economists exploring the costs and returns from alternative methods of exploitation. The concept of a bio-economic optimum has emerged as a result, and this has had due consideration in formulating international agreement on fisheries policies.

The main conceptual framework of resource economics is that

marginal cost-benefit analysis can be applied to both present and future values of a resource, provided that one has a criterion to use. The benefits from a resource are assessed for both the present generation and for future ones and Pareto optimality is assumed, that is no-one now or in the future should be worse off when the optimal disposition between all generations is considered. This approach is usually called the utilitarian one. The critical matter is to assess what the benefits will be to future generations. This is done by giving the future less weight than the present, that is future benefits are discounted by what is called an intergenerational discount rate. Governments adopt this approach; at present the United Kingdom adopts an intergenerational discount rate of about 7.5% per annum. This means that a resource valued at $100 today will have a value of only $2 in 50 years' time. The future discount rate is the keystone in the optimalising process. The higher it is the greater will be the current use of the resource. The lower it is the more that is left to future generations.

To me, and to many economists, the device of an intergenerational discount rate is repugnant and immoral. The mathematical logic employed following this first step of fixing the discount rate is impeccable, although, following the enormity of the premise, it could be regarded as an exercise in sophistry. Butlin (1981) who is an agricultural economist put this view very well. He wrote: 'If the optimal plan is for mankind to cease at some finite time in the future there is no side constraint in the criterion that would have us search for an alternative growth path, with the apocalypse approaching infinity. The fault does not lie with the criterion. It does its job which is to point out the most economically efficient growth path for an economy under a perfect institutional framework... If this calls for extinction of certain fish stocks, exhaustion of certain mineral reserves, a decline in environmental quality and the eventual destruction of the human race, *nil desperandum*: in a Pareto world all that matters is economic efficiency.' It is perhaps remarkable that Butlin did not end this passage with an exclamation mark.

Even so the utilitarian models of resource allocation, and indeed resource economics as a whole, do have merit. Such studies bring home the fact that we in our generation are in a monopolistic situation with respect to future generations. The more gloomy we are, the higher the intergenerational discount rate we will select and the greater will be our concern for the present rather than for our grandchildren.

SOME PRESUMPTIOUS REMARKS

I have the feeling that much economic theory in its conventional sense may not be as powerful a tool as many think in solving the long-term problems related to people, food and resources which we can foresee. Economics is a difficult subject, and the context of its application unbelievably complex. It has to include all those items of human behaviour which do not conform to those of a rational man in a market-place, fully informed about price and cost and motivated solely by concepts of value easily translated into money terms. These additional items include the external diseconomies, the 'irrationality' of the peasant, the absence of ownership of resources and many other aspects of human societies and individual behaviour. Imposing fabrics of theory, which are intellectually satisfying have evolved, but it does not seem that these have sufficient predictive power to enable a sure shaping of the future to be undertaken. It could be thought that these remarks do little to promote a greater understanding between biologists and economists. How they should be interpreted, perhaps, is to indicate that when dealing with problems of the magnitude of the dependence of the world's peoples on the world's resources, neither biologists nor economists have a monopoly of wisdom.

8

Solutions

A CLASSIFICATION

Many have expressed views about the problems of population and the supply of food. Their views can be roughly classified – indeed they tend to form a sequence. First are those who predict what they think will happen. Second are those who, realising the magnitude of the problems, state what might be done, without necessarily suggesting pathways to such an accomplishment. Last are those who propose specific courses of action or approaches so as to realise objectives. Obviously the latter class includes some who are concerned with generality and may well think that a particular course constitutes a panacea, as well as others who provide a more detailed guide.

That these classes reflect a sequence is perhaps illustrated by previous chapters. First there has been an analysis to suggest what might occur and this was followed by an estimate of what needed to be done – to increase food production by 75% by the year 2000. The latter is an immediate objective; little has been said about objectives in the longer term. Additionally, there has been scant mention of possible courses of action, either to meet immediate objectives or longer-term ones. It is perhaps useful to summarise what has been concluded, almost *en passant*, about the discernible future and the constraints which will beset the world's peoples, before considering possible ways in which solutions might be found.

CERTAINTIES AND UNCERTAINTIES

Despite the plethora of uncertainty surrounding estimates of the future population of the world, the basic needs of people for food, the land likely to be available for them and the limits to the productivity of that land, some stable islands of certainty have emerged from the discussions in the previous chapters. Because of the momentum of population growth, it is certain that the numbers of people in the world will increase, even if, suddenly, family size limitation became universal. Even if population did not augment, the evidence of overt malnutrition in many of the developing countries shows that there is a need for more food of higher quality. The real need is even greater than this for population will increase. Because of urbanisation, desertification and the deterioration of many irrigation systems it is certain that present farm land is being inexorably eroded and its future expansion will necessarily mean farming in a less favourable environment than hitherto and at the expense of natural resources of forest and natural grazings. It is also quite certain that there is a large gap between the average yields obtained in various countries and those which represent the potential of the crops concerned; it equally appears that these potentials will be static for many years to come. There is no doubt that yields of food could be increased; at present, however, it appears that to do so involves the use of large inputs from outside the farm, inputs which involve the expenditure of support energy, mostly derived from fossil sources.

None of these certainties about the future can be expressed in precise numerical terms. The estimate made in Chapter 5 that world food production needs to be increased by 75% in the short time to the end of the century to meet the justifiable needs of an increased population, admittedly has an air of numerical exactness. This is spurious; it was introduced simply to illustrate the magnitude of the immediate task. It is probably a reasonable estimate, but is wholly dependent on the accuracy of the original premises, namely that population will increase by a third, that the optimal supply of food energy for everyone should be that noted in western societies and that the present discrepancy between the diets in the less well developed countries and this norm is such that food output per capita in the world as a whole should be increased by a third. None of these basic premises is very precise. Compared with the declaration made at the World Food Conference in 1974 that hunger should be abolished in ten years, it has merit only in that it defines the size of the task, albeit not very precisely.

The fact that it is difficult to be precise in determining an objective for so short a period ahead, indicates the much greater difficulty of making any quantitative statements which relate to a century or more from now. Yet, if the third stage of the sequence of any study of the future – proposals for action – is to be meaningful, some estimate has to be made of the long-term needs to be satisfied. Action taken now, and designed to reach short-term goals, may well pre-empt or render nugatory some future action realised at some later time to be desirable. All that can be done, perhaps, is to state a principle rather than make any quantitative statement. This principle is that the resources of the world should be so husbanded that not only are the minimal nutrient needs of all people met, but in addition their reasonable aspirations for highly acceptable diets and for other essential products from land are catered for. Nothing is stated about some ideal number of people; it is, however, implicit in the principle that numbers must be commensurate with what food and other products can be furnished. It is thus with a quantitative statement about immediate objectives and a rather vague expression of long-term ones, that the views of many people about what might or should be done can be considered. Some of these views are discussed below, commencing with those which are extreme and indeed diametrically opposed to one another.

ABANDONMENT AND CURTAILMENT

The first group of people who have proposed solutions tend to regard the problems of population and the resources necessary to produce food as singularly related to the developing countries of the world. One of the earliest to propound the view that the developing countries should work out their own salvation was Forrester (1971). Forrester had built one of the earliest computer models of world population and it was largely as the result of this experience that he wrote, 'Instead of automatically attempting to cope with population growth, national and international efforts to relieve pressure of excess growth must be re-examined. Many such humanitarian impulses seem to be making matters worse in the long run. Rising pressures are necessary to hasten the day when population is stabilized. Pressures can be increased by reducing food production, reducing health services and reducing industrialization. Such reactions seem to have only slight effect on the quality of life in the long run. The principle effect will be in squeezing down and stopping runaway growth.'

Similar statements have been made by others. Writing of Bangladesh, Hardin (1979) commented, 'We cannot possibly keep Bangladesh afloat. To even attempt to do so would be in effect forcing greater suffering upon future generations that will inhabit the same territory.' Any who have visited Bangladesh, which is probably the second poorest country in the world, will appreciate his dismay. His view is not a new one. It reiterates that of the utterly dismal theorem as formulated by Hazlitt. Starting from different considerations, the same view has been given by others. Thus van Wazer (1978), discussing world supplies of phosphate rock, which he regarded as limiting the growth of population in the long run, stated it to be unethical 'to supply foodstuffs grown elsewhere to support rapidly growing populations in areas where they cannot support themselves'. Similar conclusions relating to the provision of aid to developing countries were reached by Lord Bauer (1984) on the basis of his economic studies in Southeast Asia and West Africa. He regards aid as not indispensible for the progress of poor countries and that its provision often prolongs the effects of damaging policies and delays development.

These views have been expressed in more popular terms and concepts. One of the latter is that of triage, a term borrowed from the battlefield, suggesting that countries, like the casualties of war should be classified into those unlikely to survive, those that could survive with immediate care and help, and those who are not so badly affected and do not require assistance. Another version is the lifeboat analogy – care must be taken not to provide too much assistance to the developing countries, otherwise in clambering aboard our lifeboat they might sink it.

TECHNOLOGICAL OPTIMISM

The alternative view, the other extreme to that of those who despair and counsel abandonment, is that which extols the ingenuity of man and his ability to plan for posterity. Again this is an old view and again it relates to Malthus' essay. Before he met Marx, Engels wrote in 1844 the following comment on Malthus: 'Has it been proved that the productivity of the land increases in an arithmetical progression? The extent of land is limited – that is perfectly true. But the labour power to be employed on this area increases along with the population; and even if we assume that the increase in yield due to this increase does not always rise in proportion to the labour, there remains a third element – which the economists, however, never consider important – namely science, the progress of which is just as unceasing and at least as rapid as that of populations . . . Science increases at least as fast as population. The latter increases in proportion to the size of the previous generation. Science advances in proportion to the knowledge bequeathed to it by the previous generation and thus under the most ordinary conditions grows in geometrical progression – and what is impossible for science?'

A modern version of Engels' statement is to be found in the conclusion reached at a conference in 1982 on Chemistry and World Food Supplies, 'We consider it vitally important that several research projects of a very fundamental nature be assigned high priority for support. If they are, then perhaps findings will be available within the next decade that will lead to increases in food production, not in inadequate successive steps of several percentage points each, but adequate increases in steps of 50%, 100%, and more. Success can by no means be promised. However, the world risks truly severe shortfalls in food production to meet both growing populations and growing expectations unless such basic programs are supported adequately in the years ahead.' (Bixler and Shemilt, 1983).

Some of the solutions which come in this category have been presented not as pronouncements of faith or exhortations for funds to pursue that faith, but in more concrete terms. Sir Alan Cottrell, for example devised a scenario in 1978 for the year 2025. He prefaced this by the passage 'it is clear that, taking the world as a whole, Man is not yet anywhere near its physical limits ... The earth's natural resources are very large, compared with Man's consumption, and any shortages we at present suffer come mainly from technological and economic limitations'. Sir Alan recognised the overriding importance of energy supplies, both for food production and for the production of other essentials. His scenario envisaged growth in the world population at 1.6% per annum, growth of energy consumption by more than double this amount – 3.5% per annum – and he concluded: 'In the scenario, enough food is provided to enable everyone to be reasonably well-fed, although not at the luxurious standards now reached in some affluent countries, and other materials and energy are also adequately provided. These provisions could all be made, given adequate forward planning to enable the necessary technology and new industries to be developed ready for when they are needed.'

There are variations on the theme. The Pimmentals (1979) suggested that by reducing the amount of grain fed to livestock in the developed countries grain would be available to meet the needs of the hungry. A little calculation shows that this would stem the tide for but a short time and the discussion in Chapter 4 indicated some of the additional considerations that have to be made if such a policy were to be adopted. The economic approach identifies the difficulties of the developing world as those of poverty rather than of resources and the solutions adumbrated are concerned with transfers of capital to help these countries emulate ourselves, again with the basic assumption that industrialisation and the development of technology will solve the problems of the pressure of people on resources necessary for the production of food.

THE INTERNATIONAL AGENCIES

Besides recipes for future action, there are many examples of contemporaneous attempts to deal with the problems that beset people and the resources on which they depend. Some have been grandiose in their conception, others more realistic. Examples of the former are Julius Nyerere's African brand of socialism – *Ujamaa* – in Tanzania, and, earlier, Kwame Nkruma's Volta River project in Ghana. More realistic ones include the many projects which have been funded by the United Nations' agencies, by other international funding bodies and by governments of the nations of the developed world. Some of these are by no means small in scale. The Mahweli dam project in Sri Lanka, which will involve the resettlement of over 1.5 million people – a tenth of the population – in new areas of the east, is hardly a small project. Neither are the plans to resettle over a million Ethiopians from the eroded highlands upon lower land small in concept. Everyone should congratulate the agencies for the effort they have made and are continuing to make. Perhaps some of the effort has been misplaced; perhaps some of the funds have been misappropriated or misapplied; perhaps expatriates who advise have received too great a share of the funds. Nevertheless, there has been an amelioration of the human condition which, while slow, would not otherwise have occurred. Criticisms abound, ranging from those which relate to details of individual projects to those which, as already discussed, condemn aid altogether. The cost of these many projects in terms of provision of capital and of immediate help is by no means small and there are many who believe that it is desirable to increase still further the provision of immediate and selective help in this fashion. Those who support the approach of increasing the aid given to countries of the developing world draw attention to the comment made by the Secretary General of the United Nations, Pérez de Cuéllar, who said, 'the total amount of official aid to all developing countries from all sources in an entire year is now equal to 18 days of military expenditure'. This statement is a sad reflection on the world's current assessment of priorities but does not diminish the effort that is at present being made in an attempt to deal with the obvious problems of the developing countries of the world. My criticism of all this effort is that the rate at which positive results accrue from it is now too slow.

This same criticism of the rates at which the problems of poverty and hunger are being removed from the world is illustrated by a speech made by Fidel Castro at the United Nations' Assembly in 1979. The speech may well not be representative of the views of most in the developing world, but it does reflect the bitterness which slow progress towards a more equitable world can generate. Castro said: 'Why must some people go barefoot so that others can drive in limousines? Why must some people live thirty-five years so that others can live seventy? Why must some be wretchedly poor so that others can be extravagantly rich? Some countries have outlets to the sea, and others don't; some have energy resources, and others don't; some are so crammed with factories that you can't even breathe the air of their poisoned atmosphere, others have nothing but their own bare hands to earn their bread. In other words, some have abundant resources and others none. What is the fate of these last? To die of hunger? To remain for ever poor? What is the use of civilisation then? What use is the conscience of mankind? What use is the United Nations? What use is the world?'

There must be some answer to this cry by Castro; something that can be done which is more than salving the conscience of the rich.

SOME PERSONAL VIEWS

My own attitude is biased towards the views of those who think that we can plan for a posterity. However poor our predictions of the numbers of mankind, the future requirements of people and the resources which will be available to meet their needs, we can identify immediate tasks and make reasonable estimates of the magnitude of longer term problems. In so doing we can state what steps should be taken to avoid the legacies that past action has bequeathed.

The first step that must be taken is to halt population increase by reducing birth rate to a rate commensurate with population stability, and in some countries to a rate which is below the replacement rate of the population, so to ensure that the surge in number due to demographic momentum is minimised. Coupled to this step is a second one, namely the relocation of populations where there is every reason to predict that numbers have outrun the carrying capacity of their environment. The third step is to provide education on such a scale that illiteracy which is the barrier to progress, can be eliminated. The fourth step is to continue the selective use of modern technology in land reclamation and in food production, searching through research and development for valid and appropriate new technologies which integrate with existing cultures. Lastly, industrial development must begin as a dispersed activity in the rural areas and must rely heavily on cooperation between developing countries, rather than be undertaken in competitive emulation of the developed world.

These proposals have been made before, either in whole or in part. Birth control and educational programmes are already in operation in many countries. There is already a large migrant force of workers attracted to the Middle East from the Indian sub-continent. An awareness of the need to improve subsistence agricultures without destruction of their social base is apparent in many of the supportive programmes being developed by international agencies. The idea that the poorer developing countries might achieve mutual programmes of industrial development towards ends which are relevant to their needs has become commonplace within the developing world. The only differences between my suggestions and these others relate to scale and speed, for the problems are immense and time is short.

IMPLEMENTATION

At the beginning of this chapter, the sequence which studies related to the future usually follow was outlined, beginning with analysis, continuing with conclusions about objectives and concluding with statements of the action that should be taken. It could be argued that the steps that I suggest represent this final phase; after all they represent positive actions likely to realise defined objectives. However, to take these steps involves untold difficulties for there are constraints at every stage. These should not be minimised. It is not sufficient to state that the People's Republic of China has through its present population policy of the one-child family shown the world that control of population is something which can be readily achieved and which can act as a model for other countries to copy. There are problems associated with this policy – of which the Chinese are only too aware. The psychological problems for the parents are real, for as was said to me in China 'an only child is very, very precious' and there are problems for the child as well. Additionally, reduction of the birth rate in such a drastic fashion creates difficulty later, when the size of the work force as a proportion of the total population falls. Quite apart from these difficulties there are those imposed by religious beliefs notably those adhered to by Catholics and Moslems and also by other denominations, who avow that birth control is sinful. Again there is resentment on the part of minority peoples at the very idea that their numbers should be controlled or curtailed. Above all there is ignorance about human fertility and its control and in many areas lack of even the most simple contraceptive devices. It is all very well to state that countries must control their populations at numbers which are commensurate with their resources and that such control should be regarded as central and continuing responsibilities of their governments. How this can be achieved is another matter entirely. Each and every country has to contend with unique circumstances which constrain the actions that might seem most logical and effective.

Again, while it seems a sensible solution to move people from lands which on all reasonable expectation can hardly support their number, there are serious difficulties in the implementation of such a step. Firstly, the ties of people to their land, however poor and unrewarding that may be, is deep rooted and there is resistance of people to change, however wretched their lot. Secondly, migrations have in the past led to the development of enclaves of those who have migrated rather than an integration, a matter exacerbated if their are racial differences between the migrants and the established inhabitants. It can be argued that since land is being taken out of production on the North American continent and since there is land in excess of population in Australasia, these countries could accept people from overpopulated and poverty-stricken areas of Central America and Asia. After all, land is fixed but people are mobile. Migration of people is just as valid a solution to the problems of population pressing too hard on resources as it was in the nineteenth century when those continents were opened to accommodate the excess population of Europe. Whether the countries concerned would accept these immigrants and whether the migrants would indeed go of their own volition are entirely different matters.

Within a modern society education is the key to the acceptance by the individual of the constraints which he must accept for the common weal. It is the key too to the adoption of sensible technologies from elsewhere, to new invention and to new initiative. The provision of education has its own problems. How far western norms and standards are relevant to developing countries is questionable, indeed is being questioned in countries which have inherited educational systems from former colonial powers. Furthermore, instruction may well be associated with indoctrination and conquest of illiteracy can be employed for a variety of ends.

All the steps thus involve difficulty, but they have to be taken if we are to make a kinder world. In some contexts some of the steps may seem draconian or as inhumane as those of triage or the philosophy of abandonment. I must emphasise again that we are in a monopoly situation as far as our children's children are concerned and it must be our purpose to provide the fabric of their future from the threads of understanding that rest in our hands. In so doing we must surely devise a new synthesis in which is incorporated not only biologically sound principles but also a humanity.

References

Ahmad, K. 1981. Effects of parasites on nutrition. *Nutrition News* (Bangladesh) 1(8)

Balba, A. M. 1983. The Asswan high dam and its impact on Egyptian agriculture. *Outlook on Agric.* 12:185–9

Bauer, P. 1984. *Reality and Rhetoric: Studies in the Economics of Development.* London, Weidenfeld and Nicholson

Bauer, P. and Yamey, B. S. 1972. *The Economics of Under-developed Countries.* Cambridge University Press

Biraben, J.-N. 1979. An essay concerning mankind's demographic evolution. *Population.* 1 (1979)

Bixler, G. and Shemilt, L. W. 1983. *Chemistry and World Food Supplies: The New Frontiers.* Toronto, Pergamon

Blaxter, K. L. 1977. Energy and other inputs as constraints on food production. *Proc. Nutrit. Soc.* 36:267–73

1981. Soils, plants and animals: The 5th Macaulay lecture. *Ann. Rept Macaulay Int. Soil Research*, pp. 138–57

Blaxter, K. L. and Waterlow, J. C. 1985. *Nutritional Adaptation in Man.* London, John Libbey

Bogue, D. 1969. *Principles of Demography.* New York, Wiley

Boserup, E. 1965. *The Conditions of Agricultural Growth: The Economics of Agrarian Change Under Population Pressure.* London, Allen and Unwin

1981. *Population and Technology.* Oxford University Press

Brody, S. 1945. *Bioenergetics and Growth.* New York, Reinhold

Buck, J. L. 1937. *Land Utilization in China.* Oxford University Press

Buringh, P., van Heemst, H. D. J. and Starling, G. J. 1975. Computation of the absolute maximum food production of the world. Mimeo, Rept Agric. Univ. Wageningen

Butlin, J. A. 1981. *Economics and Resource Policy.* London, Longman

Cabinet Office 1976. Future world trends. London, HMSO

Caldwell, J. C. and Okoujo, C. 1968. *The Population of Tropical Africa.* London, Longman

Causton, D. R. 1977. *A Biologist's Mathematics.* London, Edward Arnold

Clark, C. G. 1967. *Population Growth and Land Use*. London, Macmillan
1972. The extent of hunger in India. *Econ. & Pol. Weekly* (Bombay), September, p. 40

Clark, C. G. and Haswell, M. R. 1967. *The Economics of Subsistence Agriculture*. 3rd edn. London, Macmillan

Clark, C. G. and Munro, G. R. 1975. The economics of fishing and modern capital theory: a simplified approach. *J. Env. Econ. & Management* 2:92–100

Clark, C. and Turner, B. J. 1973. World population growth and future food trends. In *Man Food and Nutrition*, ed. M. Rechcigl, Jr. Cleveland, CRC Press

Coale, A. J. 1974. The history of the human population. *Scientific American* 231(3):41–51

Cobbett, W. 1819. *The Weekly Political Register* 34(33)

Cook, R. C. 1962. How many people have ever lived on earth? *Population Bull.* 18:1–19

Cottrell, A. 1978. *Environmental Economics*. London, Edward Arnold

Damman, E. 1979. *The Future in Our Hands*. London, Pergamon

De Hoog, J., Keyzer, M. A., Linnemann, H. and van Heemst, H. D. J. 1976. Food for a growing world population. Mimeo, Rept Agric. Univ. Wageningen

De Vries, C. A. 1973. Increasing crop yields: relative potentials of specific crops by region and/or country. In *Man Food and Nutrition*, ed. M. Rechcigl, Jr. Cleveland, CRC Press

De Wit, C. T. 1967. Photosynthesis: its relationship to overpopulation. In *Harvesting the Sun*, ed. A. San Pietro and T. J. Army. New York, Academic Press

Doubleday, T. 1847. *The True Law of Population Shown to be Connected with the Food of the People*. London, George Pierce

Dumont, R. and Mottin, M.-F. 1983. *Stranglehold on Africa*. London, Andre Deutsch

Ehrlich, P. R., Ehrlich, A. H. and Holdren, J. P. 1973. *Human Ecology*. San Francisco, W. H. Freeman

Engels, F. 1844. *Outlines of a Critique of Political Economy* [see Flew, 1970]

Eversley, D. E. C. 1959. *Social Theories of Fertility and the Malthusian Debate*. Oxford, Clarendon Press

Eyre, S. R. 1979. *The Real Wealth of Nations*. London, Edward Arnold

FAO 1950–83. *Production Yearbook*. Rome, FAO
1981. *Towards 2000*. Rome, FAO
1982. *Report of Expert Committee on Appropriate Use of Animal Energy in Africa and Asia*. Rome, FAO
1983. *The State of Food and Agriculture*. Rome, FAO

FAO/UNDF 1980. *Bush Fallow in Sierra Leone*. Rome, FAO

FAO/WHO 1965. *Protein Requirements: Report of a Joint FAO/WHO Expert Group*. FAO Nutrition Meetings Rept, Series No. 37; WHO Rept, Series No. 301. Rome, FAO; Geneva, WHO

1973. *Energy and Protein Requirements: Report of a Joint FAO/WHO ad hoc Expert Committee*. FAO Nutrition Meetings Rept, Series No. 52; WHO Rept, Series No. 522. Rome, FAO; Geneva, WHO

FAO/WHO/UNU 1984. *Energy and Protein Requirements. Report of an Expert Committee*. Tech. Rept Series. Geneva, WHO

Flew, A. 1970. *Malthus*. Harmondsworth, Penguin Books

Forrester, J. W. 1971. *World Dynamics*. Cambridge, Mass., Wright-Allen

Gilland, B. 1983. Considerations on world population and food supply. *Pop. & Devel. Review* 9:203

Golden, M. N. H. 1985. The consequences of protein deficiency in man and its relation to features of kwashiorkor. In *Nutritional Adaptation in Man*, ed. K. Blaxter and J. C. Waterlow. London, John Libbey

Golden, M. H. N. and Jackson, A. A. 1984. Chronic Severe Undernutrition. In *Present Knowledge in Nutrition*. Washington, D.C., Nutrition Foundation Inc.

Goldschlider, C. 1971. *Population, Modernization and Social Structure*. Boston, Little, Brown

Gopalan, G. 1983. '"Small is healthy", for the poor, not for the rich.' *Bull. Nutr. Foundn India*, October

Grigg, D. 1980. *Population Growth and Agrarian Change*. Cambridge University Press

Hardin, G. 1979. A biologist's concern for humanity. Quotation in *Nutrition News* (Bangladesh) 1(1)

Haub, C. and Heisler, D. W. 1980. World Population Data Sheet. New York, Population Reference Bureau Inc.

Hazlitt, W. 1807. A Reply to the essay on population by the Rev. T. R. Malthus. *Edinburgh Review*

Heal, G. M. 1981. Economics and Resources: Inaugural lecture, University of Sussex [*see* Butlin, 1981]

Hodder, B. W. 1980. *Economic Development in the Tropics*. London, Methuen

Hollingsworth, T. H. 1969. *Historical Demography*. London, Hodder & Stoughton

Holmes, W. 1977. Choosing between animals. *Phil. Trans. R. Soc. Lond. B*. 281:121–37

International Union of Nutritional Sciences 1983. Recommended dietary intakes around the world. *Nutr. Abstr. Rev.* 53:1075

Jones, H. R. 1981. *A Population Geography*. London, Harper and Row

Keyfitz, N. 1971. On the momentum of population growth. *Demography* 8:71–80

Keyfitz, N. and Flieger, W., 1971. *Population: Facts and Methods of Demography*. San Francisco, W. H. Freeman

Keynes, J. M. 1931. *Essays in Persuasion*. London, Macmillan

1933. *Essays in Biography*. London, Macmillan

Keys, A., Brozek, J., Hencschel, A., Mickelsen, O. and Taylor, H. L. 1950. *The Biology of Human Starvation*. Minneapolis: University of Minnesota Press

Knibbs, G. H. 1917. Mathematical theory of population. *J. Amer. Statis. Assn* 21:281

Lieth, H. 1973. Primary production: terrestrial ecosystems. *Human Ecology* 1:303

Lieth, H. and Whittaker, R. H. 1975. *The Primary Production of the Biosphere* New York, Springer-Verlag

Malthus, T. R. 1798. *An Essay on the Principle of Population as it Affects the Future Improvement of Society with Remarks on the Speculation of Mr. Godwin, M. Condorcet and other Writers*. London, J. Johnson in St Paul's Churchyard

1803. *An Essay on the Principle of Population; or a View of its Past and Present Effects on Human Happiness; with an Enquiry into our Prospects Respecting the Future Removal or Mitigation of the Evils which it Occasions*. London, John Murray

1830. *A Summary View of the Principle of Population*. London, John Murray

Matovinovic, J. 1984. Iodine. In *Present Knowledge in Nutrition*. Washington D.C., Nutrition Foundation Inc.

May, R. M. 1973. Time delay versus stability in populations with two and three trophic levels. *Ecology* 54:315–25

1975. *Stability and Complexity in Model Ecosystems*, 2nd edn. Princeton University Press

1981. *Theoretical Ecology: Principles and Applications*, 2nd edn. Oxford, Blackwell Scientific Publications

McHarg, I. L. 1969. *Design with Nature*. New York, Natural History Press

McLaren, D. S. 1974. The great protein fiasco. *Lancet* 2:93

1984. Vitamin A deficiency and toxicity. In *Present Knowledge in Nutrition*. Washington DC, Nutrition Foundation Inc.

McQuigg, J. D. 1981. Climatic variability and crop yield in high and low temperature regions. In *Food Climate Interactions*, eds. W. Bach, J. Pankrath and S. H. Schneider. Dordrecht Holland, O. Reidel

Meadows, D. H., Meadows, D. L., Randers, J. and Behrens, W. W. 1972. *The Limits to Growth*. New York, Universe Books

Mellor, T. W. 1976. The agriculture of India. In *Food and Agriculture*. San Francisco, W. H. Freeman

Mesarovic, M. and Pestel, E. 1974. *Mankind at the Turning Point*. London, Hutchinson

Miller, D. S. 1980. Man's demand for energy. In *Food Chains and Human Nutrition*, ed. K Blaxter, p. 23. Applied Science, London

Miller, D. S. and Holt, J. F. J. 1975. The Ethiopian famine. *Proc. Nutrit. Soc.* 34:167

Moreland, R. S. and Hazeldine, R. 1974. *Population, Energy and Growth: a World Cross-Section Study* [*see* Pearce, 1976]

Norges Landbruksvitenskapelige Forskningsrad 1984. *Energibruk og Matproduksjon i Landbruket*. Oslo, Landbruksforlaget

Odum, H. T. 1971. *Environment, Power and Society*. New York, Wiley Interscience

OECD 1979. *The State of the Environment*. Paris

Oram, P. A. 1982. The economic cost of climatic variation. In *Food Nutrition and Climate*, ed. K. Blaxter and L. Fowden. Applied Science, London

Osuntokun, B. D. 1981. Cassava diets, chronic cyanide intoxication and neuropathy in the Nigerian Africans. *World Rev. Nutrit. Dietetics*, pp. 141–202

Pearce, D. W. 1976. *Environmental Economics*. London, Longman

Pearl, R. 1925. *The Biology of Population Growth*. New York, A. Knopf

Pereira, H. C. 1974. *Land Use and Water Resources in Temperate and Tropical Climates*. Cambridge University Press

Piclou, E. C. 1977. *Mathematical Ecology*. New York, Wiley Interscience

Pimmental, D. and Pimmental, M. 1979. *Food, Energy and Society*. London, Edward Arnold

Pino, J. A., Cummings, R. W. Jr. and Toenniessen, G. H. 1981. World food needs and prospects. In *Food-Climate Interactions*, ed. J. Pankrath and S. H. Schneider. Dordrecht Holland, D. Reidel

Pirie, A. 1983. Vitamin A deficiency and child blindness in the developing world. *Proc. Nutrit. Soc.* 42:53

Pollitt, E. and Amante, E. 1984. *Energy Intake and Activity*. New York, Alan R. Liss Inc.

Poore, D. 1983. Forests. *People* 10:15

Quenoille, M. H., Boyne, A. W., Fisher, W. B. and Leitch, I. 1951. Statistical analysis of recorded energy expenditure in man. Part 1. Basal metabolism related to sex, stature, age, climate and race. *Commonwealth Bur. Nutrit. Tech. Comm.* 17

Rao, S. L. N., Adiga, P. R. and Sarma, P. S. 1964. The isolation and characterization of beta-N-aloxyl-alpha-beta-diaminopropionic acid. A neurotoxin from the seeds of *Lathyrus sativa*. *Biochemistry* 3:432–6

Revelle, R. 1976. The resources available for agriculture. *Scientific American*. September, pp. 110–21

Sadler, T. M. 1829. *Ireland: Its Evils and their Remedies. Being a Refutation of the Errors of the Emigration Committees and others touching that Country. To which is prefixed a synopsis of the original treatise to be published on the Law of Population*. London, John Murray

Schaeffer, M. B. 1957. Some considerations of population dynamics and economics in relation to the management of fisheries. *J. Fisheries Bd.* (Canada) 14:669

Schofield, W. N. 1985. The computation of equations to estimate basal metabolic rate from age, sex, height and weight. Mimeo, Rept Psychological Laboratory, Cambridge

Scrimshaw, N. S. 1977. The Atwater Lecture. *Nutrit. Rev.* 35:351

Skinner, A. 1966. *Sir James Steuart-Denby*. Scottish Economic Classics

Smith, K. 1951. *The Malthusian Controversy*. London, Routledge & Kegan Paul

Sommer, A. *Nutritional Blindness, Xerophthalmia and Keratomalacia*. Oxford University Press

Sommer, A., Hussani, G., Tarwatio, I., Susanto, D. and Soegharto, T. 1981. Incidence, prevalence and scale of blinding malnutrition. *Lancet*, pp. 1407–8

Steuart, J. D. 1767. *An Enquiry into the Principles of Political Oeconomy, being an Essay on the Science of Domestic Policy in Free Nations*. London, A. Millar and T. Caldwell; Edinburgh, Oliver and Boyd

Sukhatme, P. V. 1971. Protein strategy and agricultural development. *Indian J. Agric. Econ.* 27:1

Thatcher, A. R. 1984. How many people have ever lived on earth? *Brit. Assn Adv. Sci. Proc.* (Norwich meeting)

Townsend, J. 1786. *A Dissertation on the Poor Laws (by a Well-Wisher to Mankind)*. London

Tranter, N. L. 1973. *Population Since the Industrial Revolution: The Case of England and Wales*. London, Humanities

Truswell, A. S. 1983. Introductory Chapter: Recommended dietary intakes around the world. *Nutrit. Abstr. Rev.* 53:1075

United Nations 1953. The determinants and consequences of population change. New York, UN Department of Social Affairs: Population Division

United Nations Development Programme 1983. Development: Success stories from the UN Development Programme. *UN Chronicle* Supplement 20

University of Dhaka 1981. Protein-calorie intake as a function of land concentration. *Nutrit. News* 1:7

Van der Schalie, H. 1974. The Asswan dam revisited. *Environment* 16:9

Van Wazer, J. R. 1978. Phosphorus and mankind's problems today. In *Phosphorus in the Environment: its Chemistry and Biochemistry*, Ciba Foundation Symp. No. 57 (NS)

Walker, A. R. P. and Walker, B. F., 1981. Recommended dietary allowances and third world populations. *Amer. J. Clin. Nutrit.* 34:2319

Walker, A. R. P., Richardson, B. D. and Walker, B. F. 1972. The influence of numerous pregnancies and lactations on bone dimension in South African Bantu and Caucasian mothers. *Clin. Sci.* 42:189

Wallace, R. 1753. *A Dissertation on the Numbers of Mankind in Ancient and Modern Times*. Edinburgh

Webster, C. C. and Wilson, P. N. 1980. *Agriculture in the Tropics*. London, Longman

Whitehead, R. G. 1976. Protein and energy requirements of the UK as part of the world community. In *People and Food Tomorrow*, eds. D. Hollingsworth and E. Morse. London, Applied Science

Williamson, M. 1972. *The Analysis of Biological Populations*. London, Edward Arnold

World Bank 1984. *World Development Report 1984*. London, Oxford University Press

World Food Council 1983. Regional food priorities and security measures. *UN Chronicle* 20:8, 83

World Health Organisation 1982. Vitamin A deficiency and xerophthalmia. Tech. Rept Series No. 672. Geneva, WHO

1982. Control of vitamin A deficiency and xerophthalmia. Tech. Rept. Series No. 692. Geneva, WHO

Ziegler, P. 1976. *The Black Death*. Harmondsworth, Penguin Books

Index

Printed in the United States
By Bookmasters